A REASONABLE GOD

No matter what your situation is, or how much it changes, stay strong in your relationship with the Lord. Because you can only get a certian amount of intemecy when you spend alone Time with God.

A Reasonable God

Engaging the New Face of Atheism

GREGORY E. GANSSLE

BAYLOR UNIVERSITY PRESS

Cover Design by Andrew Brozyna, AJB Design, Inc.
Cover Image: Antique Greek Mask ©2009 Jupiterimages Corporation.
Used by permission.

Library of Congress Cataloging-in-Publication Data

Ganssle, Gregory E., 1956-
A reasonable God : engaging the new face of atheism / Gregory E.
Ganssle.
   p. cm.
Includes index.
ISBN 978-1-60258-241-5 (pbk. : alk. paper)
1. Atheism. 2. God--Proof. 3. Christianity and atheism. I. Title.
BL2747.3.G36 2009
212'.1--dc22
                  2009010374

Printed in the United States of America on acid-free paper with a
minimum of 30% pcw recycled content.

For
Eugene R. Ganssle
and
Claireanne P. Ganssle,
who taught me to love to think . . .
and everything else as well

Contents

Acknowledgments

Many people helped me along the way as this project developed. I first want to thank four former students for their encouragement: Brendan Dill, Samuel Bagg, Bryce Taylor, and Sebastian Cano-Besquet. Sebastian arranged for me to present the first version of what became chapter 7 at St. Anthony Hall at Yale University. He also gave me comments on a later version of that chapter. I am grateful that this event forced me to begin writing and for the discussion that followed my presentation. Questions raised by Troy Cross, Don Smedley, and Heidi Lockwood were especially helpful. Bryce Taylor gave me insightful comments on the first chapter. Dave Horner and Rick Schneider each read the entire manuscript with care. Both the style and the substance of the book are significantly better as a result. A variety of other friends added their two cents' worth, including David Mahan, Jon Hinkson, Jonathan Gilmore, Peter Martens, David M. Miller, Rob Tempio, Ross Miller, and Luke Potter. Bill Alston commented on the final chapter. My debt to him for this task, and for supervising my dissertation many years ago, is great. Carey Newman at Baylor University Press was an enthusiastic partner all the way through the project. My family cheered me on and provided the love and laughter that make life rich. So I thank you, Jeanie, David, Nick, and Lizzy. You bring joy beyond words.

Bits and pieces of this book have appeared in print in various places. I thank the following editors and publishers for permission to reuse material that I have published elsewhere. Parts of chapter two echo parts of my article "Copernicus, Christology and Hell: Faith Seeking Understanding" (*Philosophia Christi*, ser. 1, 20, no. 2 [1997]: 1–13). Parts of chapter 3 are adapted from chapter 15 of *Thinking about God: First Steps in Philosophy* (Downers Grove, Ill.: InterVarsity, 2004). Chapter 7 and parts of chapters 1 and 6 are adapted from "Dawkins' Best Argument: The Case against God in *The God Delusion*" (*Philosophia Christi*, ser. 2, 10, no. 1 [2008]: 39–56). Chapter 6 also contains several paragraphs from my "God and Evil," in *The Rationality of Theism* (ed. Paul Copan and Paul K. Moser, 259–77 [London: Routledge, 2003]).

I am happy to dedicate this book to my parents. I grew up in a home in which learning was encouraged, and books were part of life. My father has always had an insatiable desire to figure things out (and, in the process, to sketch numerous diagrams on napkins at the dinner table). Both of these dispositions left a deep mark on me. Long before I had heard of philosophy, my mother had to endure questions such as, "Why should I pray, if God already knows everything?" She must have given a good answer, because I still pray, and I still ask questions.

The New Face of Atheism

Questions about the existence of God have been a continuous part of the intellectual heritage of the West. Such questions have been explored by those inside and by those outside of religious belief, and they have been pursued within many academic disciplines, as well as by people in every walk of life. Recently, a number of books have been published that have taken a stance critical of religion. Because of the timing and the similarity of perspective of these works, the writers are often referred to collectively as the New Atheists. Although there may be other authors of the same ilk, the term *New Atheist* is primarily applied to four writers: Sam Harris, Daniel Dennett, Richard Dawkins, and Christopher Hitchens. Unless otherwise indicated, quotations of Harris, Dennett, Dawkins, and Hitchens are from *The End of Faith, Breaking the Spell, The God Delusion,* and *god is not Great,* respectively.[1]

These authors are called the New Atheists, but atheism itself is not new. It is instructive, therefore, to explore in what ways they bring something new to the discussion and how they stand in continuity with traditional atheism. There are three primary ways in which they capture a new approach. First, each of the New

Atheists brings a passion to their arguments that has often been lacking in more academic discussions of religious belief. These thinkers do not pretend to be neutral observers. They vigorously try to persuade their readers not only that the central claims of religion are false, but that the way we grant religion respect in our culture is misguided.

Second, the New Atheists' critique of religion involves not only the attempt to argue for the *truth* of atheism, but they aim to convince readers not to want to believe in God. These two objectives can be distinguished. Of course, if theism is false, this fact is good reason not to *want* to believe in God. The case they offer that belief in God is unattractive, however, goes beyond their arguments that there is no God. They pursue two strategies. First, they aim to convince the reader that religion is a dangerous element in the contemporary world. Second, they associate any kind of religious belief with the features of the most irrational or superstitious varieties of religion. These strategies have the effect of making religious belief undesirable before the case for or against the existence of God can be evaluated.

The third feature that reveals the New Atheists' new approach is that they occupy the position of public intellectuals. There are two ingredients to this aspect of their work. First, none of the New Atheists have entered the academic discussion of religion. They have not published academic papers or books on the topic. None of them have submitted their writings on religion to the peer-review process. To be sure, Dawkins and Dennett have extensive peer-reviewed academic publications in their areas of specialty. These areas are not related to theology or philosophy of religion, however. The second ingredient of their role as public intellectuals is their incredible popularity. It is not an exaggeration to say that the publications of the New Atheists have swept the market. Each of these books remained in the top tier of the bestseller lists for months. Furthermore, these authors have participated in numerous public lectures, debates, and television presentations of their ideas. These features distinguish the New Atheists from the long tradition of atheism in the West.

Although these writers have some largely overlapping aims and strategies, each work has its distinctive purpose. In order to engage them fairly, these purposes must be kept in mind. Sam Harris, in *The End of Faith: Religion, Terror, and the Future of Reason*, puts forward the thesis that religious belief is both incompatible with reason and the cause of a large proportion of the moral atrocities in the world. As his subtitle suggests, he is especially concerned with religiously motivated terrorism, both in the present world and throughout history. He argues that belief is the primary thing that motivates people to action, and that religious belief overwhelmingly produces evil action. He claims that people are culpable for holding beliefs that are dangerous, even if they do not perform dangerous acts. By encouraging absolute devotion and the promise of an afterlife, even a peaceful religious person can be complicit in the prevalence of religiously motivated violence.

For Harris, the answer to these problems is a proper understanding of and regard for reason. Reason will be seen to be incompatible with any kind of belief in a supernatural God. Harris does argue, however, for a rational sort of mysticism that involves the human quest for happiness. His main philosophical discussions concern three issues. First, he describes in detail what he takes to be the relation between faith and reason. Second, he challenges the notion that morality is connected in any way with religion. Third, he has a brief but important criticism of the concept of human free will.

Dennett's *Breaking the Spell: Religion as a Natural Phenomenon* is an extended argument that we ought to study religion in the same way that we study other aspects of human culture. His argument is offered in the face of what he considers to be a widespread taboo against studying the phenomenon of religion. Dennett suggests that this taboo is based on the presumption that religion, whether it embodies the truth about reality or not, plays such a vital role in culture that it would be wrong to tamper with it. The sort of study that Dennett suggests may have the effect of revealing that the underlying premise that religion plays a positive role in society is illusory.

Dennett's call to study religion as a natural phenomenon might appear to be simply a recommendation for a research project. If the recommendation is based on the assumption that religion is a natural phenomenon and nothing more, however, it is not a neutral position. And it seems clear that this latter position is the one that Dennett holds:

> I might mean that religion is natural as opposed to *supernatural*, that it is a human phenomenon composed of events, organisms, objects, structures, patterns, and the like that all obey the laws of physics or biology, and hence do not involve miracles. And that *is* what I mean. Notice that it could be true that God exists, that God is indeed the intelligent, conscious, loving creator of us all, and yet *still* religion itself, as a complex set of phenomena, is a perfectly natural phenomenon. (25; emphasis in original)

Dennett's position, in fact, is that there is no supernatural intervention in the world. Even if God exists, there is no divine revelation, and there are no miracles. God does not act on our behalf except through the laws of nature. Religion is a human invention that emerged according to the laws of physics and biology. It does not actually connect with God or any other supernatural reality. In the course of pressing his argument, Dennett offers a Darwinian story of the origin and nature of religious belief, as well as criticisms of the notion that morality is based in religion. He also articulates the relation of science to religion and criticizes various arguments for the existence of God.

Richard Dawkins' book, *The God Delusion*, is a defense of atheism in the light of current science. Dawkins' defense of atheism is multifaceted, organized around four distinct lines of argumentation. Some of his themes echo those developed in the other New Atheists. The first line of argument includes his criticisms of traditional arguments for the existence of God. He discusses cosmological arguments as well as design arguments and the notion that morality requires God in order to be sound. The second line develops explicit arguments against the existence of God. Dawkins argues, both in criticizing arguments for God and as an independent argument against the existence of God, that God requires an explanation for his own existence, as much as does the universe. Dawkins also offers the strongest argument of all the arguments against the existence of God presented by the New Atheists. He argues that the universe as we find it, with the development of life over a long process, fits better with the atheistic view than with the theistic view. As a third line of argumentation, Dawkins sketches a Darwinian account of the rise and the nature of religious belief. Both Dawkins and Dennett admit that their Darwinian stories are speculative. They do not explicitly conclude that these accounts provide evidence for atheism, although their approaches seem to be aimed at dislodging the readers' commitment to religious belief. Dawkins' fourth line includes the argument that the effect of religion in the world is and has been mostly negative. Along the way, Dawkins also explores the relation between religion and science, as well as that between faith and reason.

Christopher Hitchens' *god is not Great: How Religion Poisons Everything* argues, as its subtitle suggests, that religion poisons everything. Hitchens too thinks that religion, whether of the Western monotheistic variety or of the various Eastern versions, is incompatible with reason. Furthermore, religion is the cause of a multitude of horrors. Hitchens invests more of his work in criticizing the Jewish, Christian, and Islamic scriptures than do the other authors. He argues that these scriptures command behavior and attitudes that are absolutely immoral. Hitchens claims that what is needed is a renewal of the Enlightenment, which would refocus our energies on the fact that the "proper study of mankind is man, and woman" (283).

Hitchens engages with philosophically important arguments at a number of places. He argues that faith is incompatible both with reason generally and with the methods and conclusions of modern science in particular. He claims that the time is long past in which a religious believer can incorporate science with religious belief. In addition, he offers criticism of the design argument and the notion that morality is connected with God.

The aims of this present book are fairly modest. We will not engage all of the criticisms of religion raised by the New Atheists. We will be concerned with those that are aimed at establishing the *truth* of atheism. We will also not be concerned with defending *Christian* theism in contrast to other brands of theism. For this reason, issues concerning the historicity (or lack thereof) of the Bible or other scriptures are not explored. This book is a philosophical critique of the claim that God does not exist, as that claim is found and defended in the New Atheists. It must be emphasized that this book does not aim to put forward a comprehensive case *for* God's existence. It plays more of a defensive role. We will engage the arguments raised by these authors against the existence of God and see how persuasive they are.

The aims of this book are modest in another sense as well. Although the debate about religion can ignite passionate rhetoric, we will be concerned with providing a fair and honest engagement with the best arguments offered by the New Atheists. As we ought to expect, some of the arguments that are offered will be stronger than others. To engage them fairly requires that we admit when there are strong arguments for their position. In addition, it requires that we do not exaggerate the effectiveness of our own responses. As the following pages will show, the total case against God in these books is not compelling. Whether the reader already believes God exists or is simply wondering, she will see that belief in God is reasonable despite the best efforts of the New Atheists.

CHAPTER ONE

Science, Religion, and the Claim That God Exists

The Claim That God Exists

Before we can discuss the existence of God fruitfully, it is helpful to try to get clear what is meant by the term *God*. This aim at clarity is important because in common parlance the term has a wide variety of connotations. The task of clarifying the concept of God is not difficult. As long as we grant that there can be differences that are significant in the concepts of God that people hold, we can make headway by stipulating a concept of God. To stipulate a concept of God is not simply to assert that God is, in fact, a being with certain attributes. Rather, it is to set up a description of what God might be like and then to use this description as the starting point for our exploration. Once some kind of clarity is gained about the concept of God that is being employed, we can turn to other issues. For example, we can determine the status of the claim that this sort of God exists (or does not exist) and discover what sort of reasoning will be appropriate for the question of God's existence. We can also investigate the implications of God's existence or nonexistence for other domains of human life and inquiry.

8 — *A Reasonable God*

We can divide the possible concepts of God into a few major categories. The first distinction is between those concepts that ascribe a personal nature to God and those that do not. Clear cases of those that do will include the traditional religions of the West: Christianity, Judaism, and Islam. Clear cases of nonpersonal religions include some forms of Buddhism and Taoism. The second distinction is between monotheistic religions and polytheistic religions. Many forms of Hinduism are polytheistic, as are the ancient religions of Greece and Rome. What we call the Western religions are monotheistic. Rather than choosing from among these concepts, however, we will begin with the writings of the New Atheists themselves.

In *The God Delusion*, Dawkins claims that "a theist believes in a supernatural intelligence who, in addition to his main work of creating the universe in the first place, is still around to oversee and influence the subsequent fate of his initial creation" (18). Later he articulates what he calls the *God hypothesis*. This is the hypothesis that "there exists a superhuman, supernatural intelligence who deliberately designed and created the universe and everything in it, including us" (31). Dawkins states that he does not include personal attributes in his understanding of God because not all views of God include them. For example, deists hold that God exists and created the world but, according to Dawkins, they do not hold that God is personal. The Abrahamic faiths, Dawkins acknowledges, each embrace the concept of a personal God.

For Dawkins, the distinction between a personal and an impersonal God is located in the issue of whether or not God has a moral nature and, as a result, is concerned with human beings. Dawkins thinks the concept of God does not include a moral nature. Generally, however, philosophers and theologians have attributed the property of being personal to God if God has, at least, intellect and will—that is, if God is a being that knows things and acts for reasons. Whether God's having a moral nature is also required in order for God to be personal might be up for grabs. It is plausible to suggest that any being with sufficient intellect will have a moral nature since such a being would know whatever moral facts there are in the universe. Knowledge of these facts could be part of what provides God with reasons for acting.

On this account, even the deist God would count as personal. The deist God acts for reasons. He starts the universe because he has some reasons to do so, and then he sits back to watch. The deist God does not intervene in the universe, however. He does no miracles, and he does not reveal himself to particular human beings. It is because of these features that Dawkins calls the deist God impersonal. It is not due to a lack in God's nature (such that he lacks some attributes that would make him a person) but to a lack in his disposition.

Dennett, for his part, does not endeavor to specify what he means by the term *God*. He does, however, give a working definition of religion: "Tentatively, I propose to define religions as *social systems whose participants avow belief in a supernatural agent or agents whose approval is to be sought*" (9; emphasis in original). If the approval of the supernatural agent or agents is to be sought, then there is reason to think that the agents have some concern about human beings. At least they have enough concern to approve of us or not. So Dennett's notion of God or the gods includes their being personal in Dawkins' sense. After putting forward this characterization of religion, Dennett makes it clear that wherever the boundaries of religion are drawn, his investigation is bound to cross them.

Hitchens and Harris do not step back to articulate how they understand the nature of God. They raise the challenge that the plurality of opinions about God renders each opinion less than reasonable. We will address this objection in chapter 6. Both Hitchens and Harris do focus their attention, however, on monotheistic concepts of God. This focus is evident from their discussions of the Qur'an and the Bible, and, for Hitchens, his treatment of the traditional arguments for God's existence. These topics are relevant only to the concept of God as the creator of the world who has intellect and will and a moral nature.

Given the focus of the discussion of the authors with whom we are engaging and the long tradition in the West of thinking about the nature of God, it is fitting to stipulate the concept of God for this book as follows. I take God to be a being who is the creator of the universe. He has unlimited intellect and power, and he is a being that wills. That is, he knows all things that can be known, he can do whatever is logically possible to do, and he acts for reasons. I take it also that God has a moral nature that is wholly good.

The Existence of God as a Theory

Once a concept of God is stipulated, we can turn to the claim that God exists. It may seem at first that we should treat the existence or nonexistence of God as a theory to be investigated. Dennett raises a challenge to this treatment:

> The proposition that God exists is *not even* a theory. . . . That assertion is so prodigiously ambiguous that it expresses, at best, an unorganized set of dozens or hundreds—or billions—of quite *different* possible theories, most of them disqualified as theories in any case, because they are systematically immune to confirmation or disconfirmation. (311; emphasis in original)

There is something fundamentally correct with Dennett's proposal that the existence of God does not count as a theory. It is not because the claim is too ambiguous that it is not a theory, however. As we saw, we can remove the ambiguity by stipulating a precise concept of God. The claim that God, precisely understood, exists is a general worldview sort of claim. It allows for a variety of particular hypotheses concerning a plurality of subjects. Theories are quite specific and relate to specific questions. So, given a precise concept of God, there are still many theories about particular issues that are possible. There are different and incompatible theories about the way that moral reality is related to the nature and purpose of God or of how human beings can come to know about God or things in the world. The particular concept of God does not entail only one answer to the kinds of questions about which we form theories.

The notion that God does not exist is also too general to count as a theory. There are many different and incompatible hypotheses about the nature and origin of moral claims or the criteria for historical knowledge or the nature of the fundamental causes at work in the universe, for example, that are each consistent with the no-God hypothesis. Perhaps it is better to think of theism and of atheism as foundational claims that set parameters around the resources that are available for explaining other elements of reality. They mark out boundaries that surround families of theories about more particular detailed concerns. This fact explains why there is not just one theistic view, for example, of the nature of truth or of what is required to have justified beliefs about God. Nor is there only one atheistic view on what morality is all about or the nature of artistic experience.

Given the general level of these claims, it is no surprise that it is difficult to discern one argument or line of evidence that would definitively confirm or disconfirm either theism or atheism. The most promising strategy along these lines would be to attempt to show that there is a conceptual incoherence in claims essential to theism or to atheism. If one or the other of these positions entails a contradiction, then that position cannot be true. Attempts to find such contradictions are common in the history of philosophy, but they have been generally thought to be unsuccessful. As a result, most of the philosophical work being done currently aims at building a cumulative case for the truth of theism or the truth of atheism.

Religion as a Scientific Hypothesis—Dawkins

Dawkins insists in several places in *The God Delusion* that the God hypothesis is a scientific hypothesis, that the claim that God exists is a scientific claim. He writes, "Either he exists or he doesn't. It is a scientific question; one day we may know the answer, and meanwhile we can say something pretty strong about the probability" (48). Dawkins is emphasizing here that the claim that God exists is a claim that has a truth-value. In other words, the question of whether God exists has a definite answer, even if we disagree about it or cannot find strong reasons to hold one answer or the other. Thus he is recommending that the position that God exists is a realist position about the question of God.

There have been philosophers and theologians in recent years who have thought about religious claims in a nonrealist way. These approaches range from those with Kantian roots, such as the religious pluralism of John Hick, to the Wittgensteinian approach of D. Z. Phillips.[1] Hick articulates a view in which God is the ultimate reality, something like Kant's *thing in itself*. Each religious tradition presents its believers with mediated knowledge of that ultimate reality. No believer can claim to have unmediated knowledge of what God is like independent of human concepts. Yet each religious tradition presents its adherents with true beliefs. They are true of God as mediated within the tradition. If someone claims her beliefs describe what God is like independent of human concepts, she is mistaken.

D. Z. Phillips argues that taking the claim "There is a God" to be a truth claim in the same way as the claim "There is a book on the table" is a truth claim is a violation of the grammar of religious language. The proper grammar of religious talk focuses our attention away from metaphysical speculation about the existence or the nature of God to concerns about how we experience the world as the locus of divine activity. In a sense, when we articulate a religious claim, we are really expressing our intention to embrace a certain way of life.

By insisting that the question of God's existence is one that has a true answer, Dawkins is rightly rejecting nonrealist understandings of the nature of religion. When we claim that God exists, we are making a claim about the nature of reality. It is the claim that the way things really are includes the existence of the being we call God. The realist says, with Dawkins, that either such a being does or does not exist.

There are other places where Dawkins seems to go beyond a simple affirmation of realism. He implies that the truth of the question of God's existence has to be determined scientifically:

"Contrary to Huxley, I shall suggest that the existence of God is a scientific hypothesis like any other. Even if hard to test in practice . . . , God's existence or non-existence is a scientific fact about the universe, discoverable in principle, if not in practice" (50). Confirmation or disconfirmation of God's existence, it appears, is to be sought largely or exclusively through scientific means. Although Dawkins hints at this position, it is not his real view. Nor should it be. The question of the existence of God, he thinks, is one for which there ought to be the sort of evidence that is available to scientific methods. He does not think that scientific methods are the only ones that are relevant. The arguments Dawkins raises against the existence of God, although they draw on scientific conclusions, are primarily philosophical arguments.

Again, Dawkins is on the right track in his use of philosophical argumentation. The claim that "there exists a superhuman, supernatural intelligence who deliberately designed and created the universe and everything in it, including us" is not a claim about an empirical object. Such a being is not a physical thing, and since it is supposed to have created the universe (and it is within the universe that the laws of physics work), this being lies outside the domain of the methods of science. The scientific method cannot even pretend to encompass such a being directly. It is necessary to argue, at least in part, philosophically.

Dawkins is not unreasonable, however, to think that if God exists, there should be some empirical evidence for that fact. So even if God cannot be discovered directly by observation, there ought to be some traces of the existence of God in the universe God made that provide clues to his existence. At least some of these traces ought to be discernible by scientific methods.

The Relation between Science and Religion

Ever since the rise of modern science in the seventeenth century, there has been a vigorous discussion about whether scientific methods, or things learned by these methods, can be reconciled with religious claims. In fact, the project of reconciling science with religion (and religion with science) has a longer history that stretches back to the discussions concerning faith and reason in Augustine and the appropriation of Aristotle's physics in the work of medieval Islamic and Christian scholars. Some of the broader issues concerning faith and reason will be discussed in the next chapter. In the rest of this chapter, we will concern ourselves with science more narrowly understood and the degree to which the methods of science have applicability to questions about religion.

Stephen Jay Gould: NOMA

Both Dennett and Dawkins discuss the proposal of Stephen Jay Gould known as NOMA. This is the claim that science and religion are "Non-Overlapping Magisteria." NOMA is the position that the realms of science and of religion do not overlap at all. Each has its own subject matter, and this subject matter marks out the legitimate domain of the "magisterium." For Gould, science handles the domain of facts while religion handles the domain of values. Because these domains are completely separate, there is no room for conflict between them. Gould summarizes NOMA as follows:

> Science tries to document the factual character of the natural world, and to develop theories that coordinate and explain these facts. Religion, on the other hand, operates in the equally important, but utterly different, realm of human purposes, meanings, and values—subjects that the factual domain of science might illuminate, but can never resolve.[2]

There are two principles that make up NOMA. The first principle is that of "Equal Status of the Magisteria" (59). The second is the "Independence of the Magisteria" (63). Gould stresses the equal value of the two realms against those who are dismissive of the questions about human value and meaning. The religious realm is as important to human life as the scientific. This claim gives the book its subtitle: *Science and Religion in the Fullness of Life.* He stresses the realms' independence against those who think a proper respect for science requires reducing all human endeavors to biology, chemistry, and physics. A third aspect of NOMA is the principle by which the magisteria are individuated. For Gould, as we saw, science is the realm of fact while religion is the realm of value.

While Gould refers to religion as the realm of value, he is careful to recognize that not everyone thinks that values derive from religion. He writes,

> This magisterium of ethical discussion and search for meaning includes several disciplines traditionally grouped under the humanities—much of philosophy, and part of literature and history, for example. But human societies have usually centered the discourse of this magisterium upon an institution called "religion" . . . I most emphatically do not argue that ethical people must validate their standards by overt appeals to religion—for we give several names to the moral discourse of this necessary magisterium. (55–57)

It is not that the realm of values belongs to religion alone. In fact, the realm of values is explored throughout the humanities. Even history plays a role. The atheist who allows ethical thinking its own sphere independent of, and equal to, science is practicing NOMA as much as the theologian can. There is nothing particularly religious about the religious end of the NOMA strategy.

In fact, Gould drops hints that his proposal might evacuate religion of its specifically religious elements. Commenting on a letter by Thomas Huxley, Gould writes, "Has any 'atheist' ever presented a better case for the role of true religion (as a ground for moral contemplation, rather than a set of dogmas accepted without questioning)?" (42). Gould sets up a conflict between true religion and dogmas that are accepted without questioning. The contrast is not about the role of questioning, really. It is about the sort of religion that is legitimate. The role of religion that is legitimate is that of securing the ground for moral contemplation rather than that of providing a set of dogmas that are to be believed. Gould does not specify which dogmas he has in mind. What is certain is that the proper role of religion is restricted to issues connected with the grounding of morality, rather than those that imply there is something essentially supernatural in the realm of reality.

Dawkins and Dennett: N-COMA

Both Dawkins and Dennett are critical of Gould's attempt to reconcile science and religion. Dawkins raises several arguments against NOMA, some of which are echoed by Dennett. First, Dawkins makes the claim that even if we grant that science cannot provide the answer to every question, it does not follow that religion is the place to find these answers. There needs to be independent reason to think that religion has its own legitimate domain. For example, Dawkins admits that "we can all agree that science's entitlement to advise us on moral values is problematic, to say the least. But does Gould really want to cede to *religion* the right to tell us what is good and what is bad?" (57; emphasis in original).

Dawkins' second challenge is that NOMA sounds too much like the kind of agnosticism he rejects, *permanent agnosticism in principle.* This sort of agnosticism holds that the question of the existence of God is one for which no convincing evidence (for or against) can be had. The kind of agnosticism he thinks is reasonable is *temporary agnosticism in practice.* This sort of agnosticism withholds belief on the basis of a relative balance of evidence on either side. Dawkins rejects permanent agnosticism in principle because, as he says of God's existence, "[i]t is a scientific question; one day we may know the answer, and meanwhile we can say something pretty strong about the probability" (48). Because the question of the existence of God is one that has an answer, Dawkins thinks that it is unreasonable to insist that no reasons can be found to favor either side of the question. He thinks, in fact, that there is an overwhelming probability—due to the evidence—that God does not exist. If this claim is true, then evidence can be brought to bear on the existence of God. To subscribe to NOMA is, for Dawkins, subscribing to permanent agnosticism in principle. If we decide on principle that there is a strict boundary between the domains of science and religion, we are, he thinks, at an impasse. There is no way forward in deciding whether or not belief in God is reasonable or probable.

The third concern Dawkins raises with NOMA is that the understanding of religion required to make NOMA plausible is one that few, if any, religious people accept. He points out that "[t]he God Hypothesis suggests that the reality we inhabit also contains a supernatural agent who designed the universe and—at least in many versions of the hypothesis—maintains it and even intervenes in it with miracles, which are temporary violations of his own otherwise grandly immutable laws" (58). Religious people think that the claims they make have implications far broader than those related to providing a "ground for moral contemplation" (Gould, 42). This challenge about the way religious believers think about their own claims is raised by Dennett as well:

> Although Gould's desire for peace between these often warring perspectives was laudable, his proposal found little favor on either side, since in the minds of the religious it proposed abandoning all religious claims to factual truth and understanding of the natural world (including the claims that God created the universe, or performs miracles, or listens to prayers), whereas in the minds of the secularists it granted too much authority to religion in matters of ethics and meaning. (30)

An attempt to reconcile religion and science that reshapes religion beyond recognition turns out not to be a reconciliation at all. NOMA is a strategy of accommodation rather than reconciliation. The scope of legitimate religious claims is limited in order to accommodate the domain of science.

If Dennett and Dawkins reject NOMA, what principle concerning the relation between science and religion do they affirm? We can capture their view with a variation of Gould's acronym. They put forward what could be called N-COMA. That is, science and religion are "Nearly Completely Overlapping Magisteria." Each reluctantly grants the possibility that some questions lie outside the reach of science. Dawkins admits that "[p]erhaps there are some genuinely profound and meaningful questions that are forever beyond the reach of science. Maybe quantum theory is already knocking on the door of the unfathomable" (56). Dawkins is, as we mentioned, reluctant to grant that such questions belong to religion, and here he mentions that the realm beyond science is unfathomable. Dennett is willing to grant the possibility that religion might have a domain that is somewhat independent of science: "There may be some domain that is religion's alone to command, some realm of human activity that science can't properly address and religion can" (30).

We call their view *Nearly Completely* Overlapping Magisteria because they bring nearly every question under the domain of science. After admitting that there may be a domain for religion that is independent of science, Dennett claims, "[B]ut that does not mean that science cannot or should not study this very fact. Gould's own book was presumably a product of just such a scientific investigation, albeit a rather informal one" (30). For Dennett, even the task of discerning the boundaries of science is itself a scientific task.

Dawkins grants a more expansive role for science than does Dennett. While granting that "science's entitlement to advise us on moral values is problematic, to say the least" (57), Dawkins claims that "[t]he presence or absence of a creative super-intelligence is unequivocally a scientific question, even if it is not in practice—or not yet—a decided one" (58). He goes on to list examples of religious questions that he labels strictly scientific. The list includes, among other things, whether Jesus was born of a virgin, whether he raised Lazarus from the dead, and whether he was raised from the dead himself. "The methods we should use to settle the matter, in the unlikely event that the relevant evidence ever became available, would be purely and entirely scientific methods" (59). Dawkins does not specify how the methods of science, in particular, would help. Historical and archaeological evidence would seem to be more relevant to these questions than straightforwardly scientific evidence. Dawkins' idea about the role of science in these questions becomes clear as he summarizes his view that "miracles, by definition, violate the principles of science" (59). Presumably what science can tell us about the claim that Jesus was raised from the dead is that this event could not have occurred.

There is a connection between Dawkins' criticisms of NOMA and his idea that the question of God's existence is a scientific question. One of Dawkins' concerns is that NOMA leads us to practice permanent agnosticism in principle. He thinks that if there is no overlap between religious questions and scientific questions, then there is no way to decide rationally whether God exists or not. This concern assumes that scientific methods are the only rational methods to apply to religious questions. If there are other rational approaches to these questions, such as the approaches of philosophical or historical investigation, then subscribing to NOMA will not, presumably, stop our progress in moving from a temporary agnosticism to either theism or atheism.

Dawkins and Dennett reject all three of the claims of NOMA. They do not believe the magisteria to be entirely independent of one another. To the degree that there might be some independence, that is, that there are questions only religion or only science can address, they do not believe the magisteria to be of equal status. Third, they do not individuate the domains of science and religion in the same way that Gould does. They recognize that religious believers hold that religion makes factual claims. It is something of a revision of the religious person's own position to claim otherwise. Before I offer my own views, I will consider one other way of relating science and religion that can be called the *complementary model.*

Science and Religion as Complementary

Another approach to the relation between science and religion is that of Denis Alexander. Alexander, both a molecular immunologist and a Christian, has embraced the view that religion and science are complementary. There are different nonoverlapping levels of explanation for many of the things about which we seek knowledge. Alexander derives this model from the fact that there are multiple levels of explanation within scientific inquiry itself. For example, it is possible to talk about human digestion on the level of biochemistry and genetics as well as on the levels of physiology, ecology, and dietary science. Each level of explanation is sufficient to answer the questions appropriate to the particular level, but each also leaves unanswered a variety of legitimate questions that pertain to other levels of explanation.

Alexander expands this "level analysis" beyond the various sciences. For example, questions about human nature can be approached genetically but also anthropologically, psychologically, ethically, and, perhaps, theologically. A complete answer on the genetic level will not touch all of the issues that are raised on the psychological level. One who thinks of the various disciplines as complementary will allow each level to be legitimate and will not try to answer questions pertinent to one level with the tools appropriate to another. To mix levels or to expect the tools that are appropriate at one level to serve another is to make a category mistake.

Alexander insists on the legitimacy of the different levels: "The idea of complementarity that emerges from its use here in considering the hierarchical nature of biological descriptions carries no suggestion that the types of knowledge being related are in any sense contradictory or counterintuitive."[3] He thinks that it is simply part of reality that the sciences do not deal with every single level:

> By definition, therefore, a vast swathe of human knowledge and experience, encompassing the arts, ethics, personal relationships, philosophy and religion, lies outside the scope of science. Within this sphere of non-science, religion in particular addresses the questions of ultimate meaning and purpose and the closely related question of how we ought to live our lives. No one can escape such questions in practice because everyone has a life to be lived and, it has been argued, a metaphysical set of beliefs which are used in decision-making with regard to that

life. Scientific information tells us nothing about ultimate meaning and purpose nor gives any indication as to how we should live our lives. (*Rebuilding*, 281–82)

In some ways, the strategies of the complementary model and NOMA are similar. Both the equal status principle and the independence principle of NOMA are affirmed. The major difference is to be seen in how the domains are individuated. As we saw, Gould divides all of inquiry into two realms, that of fact and value. The complementary model claims that both science and religion can look at "the same reality from different perspectives, providing explanations that are not in any kind of rivalry to each other, but rather are complementary."[4] For the complementarian, then, it is not the subject matter of science and of religion that are independent. It is the levels of investigation, or the perspectives from which the investigation is conducted, that are independent. The distinction of the levels of investigation results in a distinction of methods as well. Alexander does not individuate his levels in the same way that Gould does. Rather, his suggestion is to look at the kinds of questions appropriate to the methods of the various disciplines. In this way, he allows for many layers of complementary research programs, not simply one of fact and another of value.

When Alexander turns to the level of religion, however, he does specify that its domain is that of "ultimate meaning and purpose and the closely related question of how we ought to live our lives" (*Rebuilding*, 282). The sciences, he thinks, cannot touch the level of meaning and morality. While this appears to reflect Gould's mode of individuation, it is important to see that the issue of meaning here is not restricted to finding meaning in our lives. Alexander claims that religion can look at empirical events and discern a larger meaning for those events by seeing them in the context of God's purposes. In a case in which someone claims that a person undergoing a medical procedure is healed in answer to prayer, Alexander says that the claims of religious discourse are "about the overall interpretation or ultimate purpose of a particular series of events and are therefore complementary to the other levels of explanation that might be provided" (*Rebuilding*, 281).

On one level, the healing occurs due to the biochemical or physiological processes that have been affected by the doctor's skill. On another level, it may be that God enabled the doctor to be successful in this case because of some larger purposes in God's mind.

Alexander's discussion of miracles also allows us to see that he is not restricting the role of religion to that of value as opposed to that of fact. He writes, "Despite Hume, science is in no position to rule miraculous claims out of court" (*Rebuilding*, 443). Alexander's recognition that scientific methods do not rule out the possibility of actual miraculous events shows that he thinks there are factual claims within the domain of religious investigation.

Assessing the Views

The two principles of NOMA and the manner of individuating the magisteria can provide the structure for a response to the attempts by Gould, Alexander, and Dawkins and Dennett to sort out the relation between science and religion. Once this response is sketched, the connection between science and the possibility of miracles will be explored.

The equal status of the magisteria is one of the central principles for NOMA. On the complementary model, as well, each level of investigation is said to be equally legitimate. The success of one set of methods for one level does nothing to support the claim that other levels are not needed or that they are less than rationally justified. Dawkins and Dennett, in contrast, are resistant to allowing that there are two separate magisteria at all, let alone that they are of equal status. If there is no God, there is no proper magisterium of religion. Part of their resistance is directly connected to their rejection of Gould's individuation of the domains of science and religion. They recognize, rightly, that religious believers think that there are religious facts. The claim that God exists or that God raised Jesus from the dead is a factual claim, as much as any scientific claim is a factual claim. These kinds of religious claims are either true or they are false. As a result, they will not reduce the role of religion to grounding value. To make such a reduction is to distort both religious claims and the domain of value itself. On the complementary model, there is no such distortion. The level of religion is as factual a level as any other.

On this point, Dawkins and Dennett (and Alexander) are right. Religious believers tend to take their religious beliefs to be claims about the way reality is. Furthermore, although religious believers often hold that religion does ground values, this statement is a truth claim about the nature of value. The realm of value, then, includes facts as well. In addition, they recognize that the realm of value is a different realm from that of religion. The irony here is that Gould, in his attempt to provide a legitimate space for religion, has had to distort it beyond what most religious people would accept. Dawkins and Dennett, in their enthusiastic criticism of religion, allow the religious believer to speak for herself about the nature of religious belief.

It appears that for NOMA and for the complementary model, more stress is laid on the equal status principle than the independence principle. These models are put forward, largely, to carve out space for religious belief. As a result, they have to stress the notion that the religious realm or level is as legitimate as any other realm or level. It is obvious in one sense that the religious level is as legitimate as any level. After all, investigating whether it is reasonable to believe in God is as legitimate an intellectual task as any. If there are good reasons to believe that God exists, then there are good reasons to think that religion connects with a realm of fact as much as other disciplines do. If one concludes that God does not exist, one will think that religious belief does not involve claims that are true. In this way, one might reject the idea that there is a religious magisterium that has equal status with the magisterium of facts or of science.

As a result of these considerations, it must be concluded that Dawkins and Dennett are correct in their rejection of the equal status principle. Given that they think there is no God in fact, they are right to think that there is no domain left for religion. It is a matter of the very taboo that Dennett wants to overcome to continue to think that religion is an independent and equal magisterium if it turns out that there is no God.

The independence principle is more interesting, especially once we grant that each level or realm involves factual claims. The claim that there is no overlap between the religious level and the scientific level requires analysis. Both Gould's and Alexander's positions raise the question of the epistemic status of the claim that religion and science belong to nonoverlapping magisteria or levels. How do we know that they belong to these completely separate realms? It is not an empirical claim that is learned from observing how the practitioners of religion or of science (or of both) actually pursue the practice of these domains. Nor is it some sort of conceptual claim, such that something about the nature of religion and the nature of science guarantees that they belong to independent domains. Neither epistemic grounding for the individuation seems to ground the claim that science and religion can never overlap.

Perhaps, then, the best policy is to adopt a view that is closer to Dawkins' and Dennett's than it is to Gould's and Alexander's. Here, the locution coined by Alister McGrath and Joanna Collicutt McGrath is helpful. They describe the relationship between science and religion as POMA, for "Partially Overlapping Magisteria."[5] Adopting POMA relieves one of having to argue either empirically or conceptually that the realms of science and religion never intersect. We can take possible intersections on a case by case basis. In some cases there may be conceptual issues that lead us to think there will be no intersection. For example, any scientific evidence for or against God's existence will be indirect. This claim is a conceptual matter concerning the boundaries of scientific methods. There will be clear cases in which we will find little to no intersection empirically. How exactly a tick's saliva works to help it suck our blood is a question that is at best only remotely connected to any theological concern. If we are considering two models for how the saliva works, theological concerns will not help us decide between them.

How would scientific and religious claims overlap? It is not hard to see how scientific claims can enter into philosophical arguments for or against the existence of God. As we shall see in chapter 4, the scientific facts discovered about the cosmic constants provide the observations for design arguments for the existence of God. In the same way, facts about animal pain can provide some of the observations that enter into arguments against God's existence. When studying God and evil, we do not separate what reasonably can be claimed about animal pain from what can be claimed about the moral nature of God. These cases are examples of overlap. The degree to which the apparent fine tuning will support a theistic argument will be determined, in part, by continued scientific study of the origin of the universe. What looks like strong (or weak) evidence at one point may be revealed to be weaker (or stronger) as our knowledge increases.

An approach like POMA also relieves us of having to think that every claim about reality must be determined based on scientific evidence. As we saw at the beginning of this chapter, Dawkins sometimes writes as if he thinks that the question of the existence of God must be answered scientifically. Dennett thinks that the proper study of religion as a phenomenon must be a scientific study. POMA will allow us to be optimistic about the contribution that scientific research can make to religious questions while allowing us to bring philosophical, historical, and other kinds of reasoning into our investigation.

Science and Miracles

We have commented that the sciences cannot encompass the being of God directly because God is not an empirical object. Any connection between scientific investigation and God will have to be indirect. A purported miracle, however, is an event in space and time. As such it is an empirical thing, and it is the right sort of thing to be subject to the type of empirical investigation that characterizes the sciences. Can the sciences show that miracles cannot occur? As we saw above, Dawkins writes, "miracles, by definition, violate the principles of science" (59).

If it turns out that miracles cannot occur, or we can never be justified in believing that a miracle has occurred, then our confidence in the truth of our religious claims may be significantly undermined. There are several questions about miracles that ought to be kept separate in order to make progress. There is the question of whether any miracle has in fact occurred. This question can be addressed to particular miracle claims. For example, we can ask whether Jesus was really raised bodily from the dead. Another set of questions is about our justification for accepting the actuality of some miracle claim. Can we ever be justified in believing a miracle has occurred? Each of these questions is important, but in this context, the question of whether it is possible for a miracle to have occurred is central. More specifically, the pertinent issue is whether science has shown or can show miracles to be impossible.

Most contemporary discussions of miracles begin with David Hume. He defined a miracle as "a transgression of a law of nature by a particular volition of the Deity, or by the interposition of some invisible agent."[6] Whether such a transgression is possible depends on what it means that something is a law of nature and what it means to transgress a law of nature. In arguing that we are never justified in accepting a report of a miracle, Hume points out that the laws of nature are established in a way that is "firm and unalterable" (114). No report, no matter how trustworthy its source, can overthrow our confidence that events take place according to the laws of nature that have been discovered.

It has often been pointed out that Hume's argument is more epistemological than it is metaphysical. The question for us, however, is not whether we can ever be justified in accepting someone's report of a miracle, but whether science rules out the possibility of a miracle altogether. Given Hume's definition, science can preclude the possibility of the miraculous only if it either establishes that there are natural laws that cannot be transgressed or if it establishes that there is no deity or "invisible agent" that stands outside those laws and can interpose its will into nature.

We have already seen that the methods of science, by themselves, cannot directly resolve the latter question. They cannot, then, show that there is no invisible agent that can intervene in the course of nature. Given this conclusion, some thinkers have claimed that either science in general or some particular science establishes that the laws of nature cannot be transgressed. The plausibility of this claim depends on what it is to transgress a law of nature. Dawkins' comment that miracles violate the principles of science is connected to this aspect of the miracles question. There are two ways to argue that science cannot allow the laws of nature to be transgressed. First, it could be argued that science has shown that there can be no exception to the outcomes determined by the laws of nature. We will call this the *metaphysical challenge*, since it is centered on the nature of reality and of the scientific laws that describe reality. Second, it could be argued that the methodologies of science require that we assume that nature is absolutely regular. In this case, the program of scientific study requires the assumption that nature is inviolable. The success of science, then, supports the claim that laws cannot be transgressed. We will call this question the *pragmatic challenge*, since it centers on the conditions for the reliability of the scientific methodologies.

The metaphysical challenge claims that it is impossible for a law of nature to be transgressed. Philosopher George Mavrodes has pointed out that there is one clear sense, at least, in which the laws of nature cannot be violated.[7] If we think of a law of nature as a kind of universal statement that all things in a particular situation will behave in a specific way, we can simplify their structure as being of the form "All A's are B's": for example, "All dead people stay dead." If some event turns out to be a counterexample to this statement, then the statement is not really a true law of nature. If we find an A that is not a B, then the sentence "All A's are B's" turns out to be false. If someone is raised from the dead, then the statement that all dead people stay dead is shown to be false.

What we need is to understand laws of nature in a more restricted sense than that of a universal claim. Mavrodes solves this problem by showing that statements of the form "All A's are B's" are not the laws of nature themselves. Rather, they are generalizations that are associated with laws of nature. They express what normally happens. Normally, all A's are B's. He explains that such a generalization "would be a true description of the world *if nothing outside of the natural order interfered with the operation of the corresponding law of nature*" (309; emphasis in original). So the generalization "All dead people stay dead" is still true even if someone was raised from the dead. The generalization is made in the context of a noninterference assumption.

That laws of nature involve a noninterference assumption can be seen by the requirement that laws hold for closed systems. The claim that energy in a system is neither created nor destroyed entails that the total energy in a system will remain constant provided it is a closed system. Suppose a person designs an extremely sensitive experiment to confirm the principle of the conservation of energy. If someone else comes along and shines a light into the experiment, it will be ruined. The light does not falsify the conservation law. It ruins the experiment by introducing more energy into the system. The possibility of interference from other factors (or other human beings) is one of the main problems encountered in executing experiments in controlled situations. We try to control the situations to eliminate the possibility of interference.

The concept of a miracle includes the concept of interference. It is not that the laws of nature are suspended, but that the noninterference condition is overridden. In the case of a miracle, the noninterference assumption does not hold. The universe is not a closed system if miracles are possible. All dead people stay dead if no agent of sufficient power intervenes to raise someone from the dead. No matter how well the laws of nature are established, they cannot rule out the possibility of interference. The metaphysical challenge, then, fails. Miracles are not incompatible with the sciences.

The pragmatic challenge to the possibility of miracles focuses on the idea that the reliability of scientific methodologies requires the truth of the noninterference assumption. In order to do scientific investigation with any hope of making progress we must assume there will be no interference. Allowing the possibility of divine interference, then, undermines the integrity of the scientific enterprise.

This concern is an important one. Unless we have a firm expectation that there will be no interference, we will not make progress in our scientific investigation. We can see the strength of this challenge by imagining the following situation. If one percent of all events in the universe involved divine interference, it would be impossible to make any secure generalizations about how events normally unfold. Under these conditions, it is possible that modern science would never have gotten off the ground. What is required for a robust scientific research culture is a firm system of regularities.

It is not only scientific research programs that are invested in the regularities of the laws of nature. All of our knowledge of the world depends upon regularities. If the physical world were not stable, we could not navigate it. We could not find food and water (and what counted as good food and water at one time might not count as such at another time). The regularity of the physical world is a deep assumption by which everyone lives. Significant interference, even if it amounted only to one percent of events, would render everything chaotic. Yet the proponent of miracles is opening the door to precisely this kind of interference.

The answer to the pragmatic challenge involves admitting that these concerns are legitimate. The concept of a miracle does involve interference. What violates the presumption of regularity is widespread interference. In order for the miraculous not to undermine this presumption, it has to be exceedingly rare. It is probably impossible to pick out the exact percentage of events that must be regular in order for our presumption not to be undermined. There will be clear cases, however, of percentages that are too high to maintain our presumption and percentages that are low enough to maintain it. If one in one hundred events is a case of divine interference, our presumption of regularity is undermined. If there have been only seven miraculous events in the history of the universe, our presumption of regularity is safe.

If we are correct about both the metaphysical and the pragmatic challenges, then science cannot rule out the possibility of the miraculous. It will generate a strong presumption that any particular event is not miraculous. We will need good reason to conclude that any particular event is miraculous. We shall not explore the kinds of reasons that would be relevant here. If there are good reasons to think God exists, however, then there are good reasons to think it likely that some miraculous events have occurred. God's existence does not require that miracles have occurred, but it does make it somewhat likely. A big part of determining whether any particular event is miraculous, then, is the background investigation into the reasonability of thinking God exists.

We have seen that the methods of science cannot encompass God directly, although it is reasonable to expect that, if God exists, there will be scientifically assessable evidence for this fact. Such evidence will enter into arguments for (or against) his existence. The arguments themselves will not primarily be scientific, contrary to Dawkins. The case for or against God's existence will be largely philosophical.

CHAPTER TWO

Faith, Reason, and Evidence

One challenge often raised against religious belief is that of reconciling faith and reason. There are two major sources for this challenge. First, it appears to many people that religions ask their followers to accept doctrines without providing good reasons for them to do so. This posture is thought to render religious beliefs irrational. Our most important beliefs ought to be supportable by or grounded in good thinking. Good thinking requires the use of reason to be primary. Second, it is widely believed that it is impossible to prove that God exists. This idea leads many people to think that religious belief can be a matter only of faith. Reason appears to have no bearing on how religious people acquire or maintain their beliefs about God.

Harris on Faith and Reason

Each of the New Atheists raises some of these concerns. Sam Harris' book *The End of Faith*, in particular, could be summarized as a sustained attack on the very notion of faith. The bulk of his work argues that living by faith motivates believers to do things that range from the stupid to the dangerous. Apart from this main worry, Harris also is concerned that faith precludes reason by its very nature. He claims, for example:

> Whatever their imagined source, the doctrines of modern reli-
> gions are no more tenable than those which, for lack of adher-
> ents, were cast upon the scrap heap of mythology millennia ago;
> for there is no more evidence to justify a belief in the literal exis-
> tence of Yahweh and Satan than there was to keep Zeus perched
> upon his mountain throne or Poseidon churning the seas. (16)

Harris thinks that religion cannot be supported by reason. He writes, "[E]very religion preaches the truth of propositions for which it has no evidence. In fact, every religion preaches the truth of propositions for which no evidence is even *conceivable*" (23; emphasis in original). This claim can be read in two ways. First, it appears that Harris is claiming that religious belief by its very nature cannot be supported by any evidence at all. On this read-ing, it is not that the evidence that religious believers put forward is insufficient. It is simply impossible for there to be evidence. A second possibility is that he does not mean to indict every propo-sition included in each particular religion. He might be claiming that each religion is such that there are some claims it asks us to believe for which no evidence is conceivable.

The first interpretation puts a much stronger claim into Har-ris' mouth: religion by its very nature cannot be supported by any conceivable evidence. This kind of claim has been made in the past. For example, in the middle of the twentieth century, analytic philosophy was dominated by logical positivism. The logical posi-tivists, in short, held that a statement or a sentence is meaning-ful only if it is either a tautology or if it is empirically verifiable. On this view, religious claims, as well as ethical and metaphysical claims, were not meaningful. They were not false. They did not even make an assertion that could be true or false. Therefore, they were the sort of claims for which no evidence could be conceived.[1] Although logical positivism has been revealed to be incoherent, it is important to remember that the idea that religion is strictly out of the reach of evidence is not without historical precedent.

On the second interpretation, Harris is making the weaker claim that each religion includes some doctrines that are not supported by the kind of evidence Harris thinks is necessary. Some religious claims are supported by other beliefs held within the particular religious system. For example, a Christian might believe that Jesus genuinely predicted the future when he told Peter that Peter would deny him.[2] If the believer is asked why she holds this to be true, part of her reason might involve other beliefs within Christianity, such as the claim that Jesus was fully God as well as fully human. The claim about Jesus' divine identity is not the sort of evidence with which those who are not Christians are satisfied. So it might be that Harris would consider the belief that Jesus genuinely predicted the future as an example of a claim for which no evidence is conceivable, while the Christian supports it with other beliefs she thinks are well grounded.

Harris does lay out his criteria for reasonable belief formation:

> With each passing year, do our religious beliefs conserve more and more of the data of human experience? If religion addresses a genuine sphere of understanding and human necessity, then it should be susceptible to *progress;* its doctrines should become more useful, rather than less. Progress in religion, as in other fields, would have to be a matter of *present* inquiry, not the mere reiteration of past doctrine. Whatever is true now should be *discoverable* now, and describable in terms that are not an outright affront to the rest of what we know about the world. (22; emphasis in original)

It appears that, in order to be well-supported evidentially, religious belief has to be the sort of body of belief that progresses. There must be new things added to religious knowledge. While this claim might be challenged, the more important statement is, "Whatever is true now should be *discoverable* now . . . ." Presumably, Harris is claiming that if it is true that God exists, it ought to be discoverable now that he does. The claim that whatever is true now is discoverable now, however, is clearly false. This standard is not held in any other field of study. There are mathematical statements that are now true but not discoverable until they are proven. These statements do not become true when they are proven. Many scientific claims that are true are, as of yet, outside the reach of our knowledge. This fact provides part of the motivation for continued research. There are trivial claims about the past that are true but will never be discovered. Consider the following two sentences: With his own hand, the total number of words Isaac Newton wrote was odd. With his own hand, the total number of words Isaac Newton wrote was even. One of these sentences is now true. It very well could be that it is impossible ever to determine which of them is the case. Harris' contention that we ought to be able to settle the question of the truth of religion now is not well grounded.

Hitchens on Faith and Reason

Christopher Hitchens also thinks that religion cannot be based on reason. He does not hold, however, that it is the very nature of religion that precludes reason. Hitchens thinks that the development of what we know about the world renders religious belief irrational. He claims, "Faith of that sort—the sort that can stand up at least for a while in a confrontation with reason—is now plainly impossible" (63). We might well ask why a faith that can "stand to reason" is *now* impossible. Hitchens claims that we know that a reasonable faith is impossible from observing the origin of religious belief:

> Religion comes from the period of human prehistory where nobody—not even the mighty Democritus who concluded that all matter was made from atoms—had the smallest idea what was going on. It comes from the bawling and fearful infancy of our species, and is a babyish attempt to meet our inescapable demand for knowledge (as well as for comfort, reassurance, and other infantile needs). Today the least educated of my children knows much more about the natural order than any of the founders of religion, and one would like to think—though the

connection is not a fully demonstrable one—that this is why they seem so uninterested in sending fellow humans to hell. All attempts to reconcile faith with science and reason are consigned to failure and ridicule for precisely these reasons. (64–65)

It is because religion originated in the ignorant infancy of the human race that reconciliation with science or, more generally, with reason can now be seen to be impossible. Presumably, there was a time when religious belief could be reconciled with the "current" science. Perhaps Hitchens would think that Aquinas' integration of Christian philosophy and theology with the philosophy and physics of Aristotle is an example of this kind of reconciliation. Since the rise of modern science, he seems to argue, that sort of integration has been shown to be impossible.

These claims too can be challenged. First, it would be good to have an idea of when the period of the "bawling and fearful infancy of our species" took place. Christianity, for example, began two thousand years ago, centuries after the rise of philosophy, geometry, and democracy. One could respond that while the distinctives of Christianity are two thousand years old, the religious impulse itself dates from the ignorant infancy of the human race. Of course, the impulse to understand the world also dates from the same time. It can be argued, furthermore, that modern science also originated in a period of relative ignorance. The historical time frame of the origin of a domain such as religion or science (or mathematics or art) is not a reliable guide to the potential for a reasonable defense of the central claims of that domain. Those claims themselves must be subject to investigation in order to determine whether or not they stand to reason.

Hitchens' primary concern is probably not about the historical period in which religion emerged. It seems that his view is that what we learn from science has rendered rational belief in God impossible. The historical argument he is putting forward is that it is no longer possible to reconcile religion and reason. Science, he seems to think, shows that the claims of religion are false or, at least, not supportable. Therefore, in recent centuries, it has become impossible to reconcile reason and religion.

There are two kinds of responses that are appropriate. In chapter 1, we looked at what exactly science can and cannot say about religious claims. It turns out that the domain of science and the domain of religion are not completely independent, but that science cannot challenge directly most religious claims such as the possibility (or the actuality) of miracles or of the existence of God. Second, the fact that science as a whole cannot rule out the existence of God or the reality of miracles does not imply that particular scientific claims cannot challenge (or support) particular claims or theories of some religions. The interaction between particular claims and theories has been fruitful. That there is a conflict between particular claims, however, must be established on a case-by-case basis. Sound procedures for this sort of investigation will be explored below.

Dawkins on Faith and Reason

Dawkins is less sure that reason can play no role in religion than is Harris or Hitchens. As we saw in chapter 1, Dawkins insists that the claim that God exists be treated as a "scientific claim." We found that, while the claim that God exists is not itself an empirical claim, it is a claim that has a truth-value and ought to be tested by appropriate means. Dawkins allows that evidence for the existence of God is possible. His view of the possibility of evidence is revealed in his discussion of the kind of agnosticism that he thinks is reasonable. He rejects permanent agnosticism in principle precisely because the question of God is one for which evidence ought to be expected one way or another. Because the question of the existence of God is one that has an answer, Dawkins thinks that it is unreasonable to insist that no reasons can be found to favor either side of the question. He thinks, in fact, that there is an overwhelming probability—due to the evidence—that God does not exist. If this claim is true, then evidence can be brought to bear on the existence of God.

Although Dawkins frames this distinction in the context of kinds of agnosticism, it can apply to atheism as well. We can wonder whether Hitchens or Harris is the sort of atheist that Dawkins might be rejecting here. Hitchens seems to hold that the impossibility of evidence only applies to those who want to support the existence of God. He thinks there is plenty of evidence for the claim that God does not exist. In fact, he seems to argue, in the passage cited above, that the whole tenor of scientific knowledge counts as evidence against the existence of God. What remains problematic about Hitchens' view, in contrast to Dawkins', is the notion that there is evidence for one side of a dispute but that no evidence is even possible for the other.

Harris, however, might be the sort of atheist in principle that Dawkins rejects. As we saw, whether he is or is not depends on what he means by the claim that no evidence is even conceivable for religious claims. This statement can be taken to mean that Harris thinks that the evidence against the existence of God that is provided by "science" is so overwhelming that it is not conceivable that other sources of evidence could counter it successfully. In this case, he would not be one who holds permanent atheism in principle. A fully convinced atheist need not be a permanent atheist in principle. Harris would be the sort of atheist Dawkins rejects only if Harris' claim means that every religious claim is by its nature outside the domain of any evidence.

Dawkins does think there is something about religious faith that is different from believing a theoretical claim on the basis of evidence. He writes, "It is in the nature of faith that one is capable, like Jung, of holding a belief without adequate reason to do so . . . Atheists do not have faith . . . " (51). Atheists do not have faith because, presumably, they have evidence for their claims. Dawkins maintains this distinction by insisting that science does not require faith. Again, the mark of what counts as scientific is that what is believed in science is believed based on evidence, and that scientific beliefs are revisable in light of new evidence. Dawkins insists that his "belief in evolution is not faith, because I know what it would take to change my mind, and I would gladly do so if the necessary evidence were forthcoming" (283).

Dennett on Faith and Reason

Dennett too sees that evidence is possible both for and against religious belief. He writes about religious people, "They may be right, but *they don't know*. The fervor of belief is no substitute for good hard evidence, and the evidence in favor of this beautiful hope is hardly overwhelming" (16; emphasis in original). Dennett repeats the insistence at a number of places that religious believers do not know that they are right:

> Who is right? I don't know. Neither do the billions of people with their passionate religious convictions. Neither do those atheists who are sure the world would be a much better place if all religion went extinct. There is an asymmetry: atheists in general welcome the most intensive and objective examination of their views, practices and reasons . . . . The religious, in contrast, often bristle at the impertinence, the lack of respect, the *sacrilege*, implied by anybody who wants to investigate their views. (16, 17; emphasis in original)

Although Dennett claims that neither the theists nor the atheists know they are right, he thinks there is an asymmetry between them. Only the latter welcome objective examination of their views.

This claim about the relative willingness to have their views examined is a generalization that might not be accurate. The degree to which it applies might be relative to the cultural context. For example, there are many contexts in which it well might appear that religious believers are not open to objective examination. These contexts might be when the religious believers are in the majority. In the secular academy, however, religious believers often have their beliefs challenged. Because religious believers are in the minority in the university, they are accustomed to critical engagement about their beliefs.

Dennett thinks that many believers and even some atheists are more caught up with "belief in belief" than with belief in God. Belief in belief emerges when a person thinks that belief in God is valuable regardless of whether or not it is true or well grounded. Many people seem to think that widespread religious belief is necessary for civil society, for example. If someone thinks that religious belief is necessary to society, even if it is false, then she has belief in belief. For such people, the value of religious belief extends beyond its truth. People who have a strong belief in belief will generally not be open to an objective examination of such views. Dennett writes, "Belief in belief in God makes people reluctant to acknowledge the obvious: that much of the traditional lore about God is no more worthy of *belief* than the lore about Santa Claus or Wonder Woman" (210; emphasis in original).

Another problem with religious belief, according to Dennett, is that the content of religious belief is supposed to be beyond reason in some way. "The fundamental incomprehensibility of God is insisted upon as a central tenet of faith, and the propositions in question are themselves declared to be systematically elusive to everybody" (Dennett, 220). He has drawn attention to the importance of sorting out the requirement for evidence on the one hand and the nature of the content of religious belief on the other.

Sorting Out Faith, Belief, and Evidence

The difficulty of bringing religious faith into some kind of harmony with reason, then, is one of the challenges the New Atheists lay at the feet of religious believers. Unless some kind of position can be articulated that allows religious belief to be reasonable, belief in God will not have much to recommend it, that is, much to recommend it rationally. The first step to take to bring faith and reason together is to clarify some of the ambiguities in our use of terms such as *faith, belief,* and *reason*.

The term *belief* is used in two ways that require disentanglement. First we talk about what we can call *belief that*. We believe that certain things are true. For example, I believe that rain is composed of water, that the battle of Gettysburg was completed before the year 1865, and that it is wrong to torture another human being for no particular reason. These claims constitute some of the content of my various beliefs. To believe that these items are the case is to take them to be facts. I take them to be facts, even if it turns out that they are not actual facts. I could be wrong about what I take to be a fact even if, as in these cases, it is not likely. Harris recognizes this use of the term. He sees that religious believers do hold truth claims about the world. He explains in more detail what it is to believe that something is the case:

> Believing a given proposition is a matter of believing that it faithfully represents some state of the world, and this fact yields some immediate insights into the standards by which our beliefs should function. In particular, it reveals why we cannot help but value evidence and demand that propositions about the world logically cohere. (51)

To *believe that*, then, is to hold that the content of your belief faithfully represents some state of the world. Various instances of believing that something is true will be similar, regardless of the content of the belief in question. As a result, we can sort out what makes something a good case of *believing that* and what makes it a bad case of *believing that*. While there may be some cases that are not clear, there are plenty of clear cases on either side. From these cases, we can try to discern principles that mark the good cases and principles that mark the bad ones.

The other use of *belief* can be captured by the phrase *belief in*. To *believe in* something or someone is more than to believe that some claim is true. It is to trust or to have confidence in or to be in favor of that thing or person. We use this term in a variety of senses, such as "I believe in recycling" or "I believe in telling the truth" or "I deeply believe in my wife." These English phrases can still be ambiguous. Sometimes we use the words *believe in* when we really mean we *believe that*. We can clarify them by articulating which we mean. If I say, "I believe in God," I may mean that I believe that it is true that God exists, or I may mean that I trust in God as an important part of my life. Religious believers usually both believe that God exists and believe in God.

The distinction between *belief that* and *belief in* helps us sort out our evaluation scheme. We could say that the aim of *believing that* is truth. We want to believe that something is the case only if it really is the case. Evaluating *belief that*, therefore, requires figuring out which ingredients of *believing that* are truth conducive. *Believing in*, however, has a different aim. It is not primarily about tracking the way the world is. It is more focused on desiderata such as reliability, worthiness, or sound policy. So, to say that I believe in recycling does not mean I think recycling is true. Nor does it mean simply that I believe recycling is good for the environment. It means that I also practice recycling. To say I believe in telling the truth is to say more than I believe that it is better to tell the truth than not to. When I express that I believe deeply in my wife, I mean that I have a deep and abiding confidence in her character and friendship.

Notice that when we unpack what these statements mean, it becomes clear that *believing in* is related to *believing that*. The fact that I believe in my wife, or in telling the truth, or in recycling involves that I believe that certain things are true. I believe that she is trustworthy. I believe that telling lies is wrong. I believe that recycling is good for the environment. These *belief thats* serve as some of my grounds for my *belief ins*. That I have grounds for a case of *believing in*, however, does not automatically make it the case that I believe in those things. A person can believe that recycling is sound policy without believing in recycling. Such a person may hold that the claim that recycling is sound policy is true, while for some reason he continues to refuse to recycle.

The connection between *believing that* and *believing in* is not completely proportional, however. Rational *believing in* does not track rational *believing that* exactly. There is a common claim that one ought to proportion one's belief to evidence. While this claim might be applicable to cases of *believing that*, there are many counterexamples to its use in cases of *believing in*. *Believing in* often cannot be proportioned to the grounds for the corresponding *believing that*. For example, I often get into my car and drive on I-95 in Connecticut. All of the available evidence convinces me that there is a less than 100 percent chance of reaching my destination safely. While I may be able to proportion my *belief that* to the evidence, my *belief in* will be either 100 or 0 percent. Either I get in the car and drive on I-95, or I do not. I cannot get in the car 99 percent. While it may be possible to proportion my commitment to my wife to the evidence of her love for me, it is a bad marriage policy to do so. Rather, I continue to believe in her love for me with a total commitment, even if one could produce a small bit of evidence to the contrary.

One thing that bothers many people, including some of the New Atheists, about religious believers is that they seem not to proportion their belief to the evidence. If it is the case that the evidence that God exists is strong but not strong enough to deliver certainty or to eliminate all reasonable doubt, then a person might come to the conclusion that it is likely or more probable than not that God exists. Such a person might go beyond believing that God exists and begin also to believe in God. His *belief that* might be proportional to the evidence but his *belief in* involves the sort of personal commitment that cannot be proportioned. Making this commitment is warranted based on evidence, but the level of commitment goes beyond evidence (and does so reasonably). In this way, believing in God is more like a marriage relationship than an academic exercise.

Believing Based on Evidence

Much of the discussion among the New Atheists about the irrationality of religious belief centers on the issue of evidence. In epistemology, discussions about evidence generally take place within a broader discussion about the nature of the justification or the grounding of beliefs. One reason that it is important to have an account of justification is that justification is thought to separate cases of genuine knowledge from lucky guesses. A person may have a true belief about something, but he may have this belief only because it is a hunch. So if someone is looking for her keys, her friend may believe that they are in the car. If it turns out that he is right, we do not say that he knew her keys were in the car. Before we would say that he knew they were in the car, we would want to know why he believed they were. If he just had a hunch, not based on any other reasons, then his true belief was more of a lucky guess than genuine knowledge. If, however, he saw them in the car, then his belief might very well count as knowledge. In both cases, he has the same true belief. In the first case, that belief did not count as knowledge. In the second it did.[3]

We can use the term *evidentialism* for the view that a belief that something is the case is justified for a person only if that person has sufficient evidence for it. Evidentialism is one view of the nature of justification.[4] Evidentialists hold that most beliefs are justified by propositional evidence. That is, they are justified if they are "properly" based on other beliefs that the person is justified in holding. For example, my belief that tigers are not indigenous to Africa is based on other beliefs I have, including my belief that the books I read as a child generally told the truth. If my belief about the books I read was not justified, then my belief about tigers would not be either. Some beliefs, such as my belief that I had eggs for breakfast, are justified based on evidence that is not propositional. My memory experience can count as evidence, even if that experience is not itself another belief that I have. Some theists will include belief in God as the kind of belief that can be justified independent of evidence. This belief is analogous, they say, to our beliefs in the existence of other minds, in the reliability of sense perception, or in the reliability of memories.[5]

In what follows, we will not defend a theory of justification. Nor will the view that belief in God can be justified independent of evidence be explored. Rather, we will assume that some form of evidentialism is the case. In order for a person to be justified in holding some belief, she must have sufficient evidence for it. We will make this assumption because it is the same one made by each of the New Atheists. The two questions that emerge, then, involve what counts as evidence and what counts as sufficient evidence.

What Counts as Evidence?

If the existence of God requires evidence, it is important to investigate what could count as evidence for this kind of claim. We saw in the previous chapter that not all evidence for or against the existence of God will be empirical evidence. The existence of God is a metaphysical claim, and therefore it requires evidence of the sort provided by metaphysical argument. Harris has some helpful points in considering the nature of evidence. He explains that "evidence is simply an account of the causal linkage between states of the world and our beliefs about them" (62). He explains in more detail what he means by the causal link:

> To believe that God exists is to believe that I stand in some rela-
> tion to his existence *such that his existence is itself the reason for*
> *my belief.* There must be some causal connection, or an appear-
> ance thereof, between the fact in question and my acceptance
> of it. In this way, we can see that religious beliefs, to be beliefs
> about the way the world *is*, must be as evidentiary in spirit as
> any other. (63; emphasis in original)

Harris is right that there must be some kind of connection between what is taken to be evidence and the belief in question, but some causal links will not count as evidence. For example, suppose God exists and he causes me to be hit in the head with a baseball. One of the results of this event is that the neurons in my brain are affected such that the belief that God exists is formed within me. In this scenario, there is a direct causal link between the fact of God's existence and my belief in it. This link is not evidentiary, yet it may satisfy Harris' criterion that "I stand in some relation to his existence *such that his existence is itself the reason for my belief.*" In this case, God's existence is the reason that I believe in him but it does not provide me a good reason to believe in him. The relation between evidence and belief has to be more than causal.

Another problem is that Harris' account does not allow there to be evidence for a false belief. Evidence, he claims, is a relation between a person's belief and the fact that the evidence supports. If someone has reasons to think God does not exist, even though he does, these reasons should still count as evidence. If Harris is right about the nature of evidence, however, no one can have evidence for God's nonexistence. If God does exist, then none of the atheist's reasons are caused by the way the world actually is.

Harris is trying to get at two important features of the nature of evidence. Evidence must be both truth-conducive and reason providing. Evidence for a claim must make it more likely that the claim is true, and it must provide the person who believes the claim with reasons to think that it is true. These two features help resolve the two problems we found with Harris' explanation of evidence. First, the fact that God hits me with a baseball implies that he exists but it does not give me (the one who is hit without knowing that God is doing the hitting) a reason to think so. Second, there can be evidence that God does not exist, such as a particular version of the problem of evil, even if it turns out that he does.

The possibility of having evidence for a false belief highlights the fact that, in philosophy, most major claims or theories are supported by cumulative cases. Various lines of evidence together point either toward or away from a theory. Some lines of evidence, when taken in isolation, might be fairly strong even if the total case points in the other direction. Recognizing this fact allows the thinker to be more generous to claims with which he disagrees. One can grant that a particular argument renders the existence of God more probable than it would otherwise be, even if one thinks that the total case strongly supports atheism.

What counts as evidence for a person is whatever raises the likelihood for that person that the claim is true. Evidence is, as we said, truth conducive. Evidence for God's existence (or nonexistence) does not have to be restricted to empirical findings discernible in the sciences, although some empirical findings might serve as evidence. The evidence will be found mostly in the form of philosophical arguments.

What Counts as Sufficient Evidence?

It is tempting to think that evidence for religious belief must reach a higher standard than evidence against religious belief. In fact, it is tempting to look for proof or certainty that God exists. Most of the arguments for God's existence were originally framed as proofs because the thinkers, such as Thomas Aquinas, thought they succeeded as proofs. The overwhelming consensus of phi-losophers has been that Aquinas' arguments, as well as any of the other arguments for God's existence, fail as proofs. The degree to which the arguments support their conclusion is less than one hundred percent. In fact, it has become somewhat a cliché that God's existence cannot be proven. Dawkins correctly shifts the discussion to one of probability: "What matters is not whether God is disprovable (he isn't) but whether this existence is *probable*" (54; emphasis in original).

Another reason that many people insist on a higher standard of evidence for religious claims is that they think the atheistic position is neutral. Therefore, the theist requires a stronger case on his behalf. Neither the atheist nor the theist is in a neutral posi-tion, however. Each holds a theory or elements of a theory about the nature of the universe. As such, the burden of proof ought to be thought to be equivalent between the two positions.

An agnostic might think that he is in a more neutral posi-tion than either the theist or the atheist. The sort of agnostic that Dawkins calls the permanent agnostic in principle, however, is not at all neutral. She holds that the question of God's existence can-not ever be decided based on the evidence. This position is itself made up of claims that require defense. One who holds tempo-rary agnosticism in practice is the sort of agnostic who is assessing the evidence in order to land either in the theistic or the atheistic camp. This position might be closer to being a neutral one. Tem-porary agnosticism in practice, however, is not a position within which one can rest. The goal of the temporary agnostic is not to remain agnostic but to find enough grounding to believe reason-ably in the existence or in the nonexistence of God. As such, the one who holds to temporary agnosticism is in a temporary posi-tion. She aims to shift into another, less neutral, view.

The fact that there is no stable neutral position and that there is little chance of a proof on either side help us recognize the guide-lines for our standards of evidence. If we are deciding between two theories (atheism and theism) then the strength of the evi-dence only has to be recognizably stronger for one side than for the other. To talk about "recognizably stronger" evidence for one side over another is admittedly vague. It cannot be specified precisely what would count as recognizably stronger evidence, but we can sort out some clear cases. For example, one could have recognizably stronger evidence for one's views even if one grants that there is evidence against them. A person can believe, therefore, that there is recognizably stronger evidence for theism even if she holds that it is reasonable for some people to be atheists. On the other hand, it would not be reasonable to call the evidence for one side recognizably stronger if the difference in evidence amounts to something like a 51 percent/49 percent distribution. This distribution would be too close to call. In this way, there is an area in which we would call the evidence more or less equal for either claim. In this range, the question of God's existence might be too close to call.

A further question that can be raised is this: to whom must the evidence be recognizably stronger? The evidence must be recognizably stronger for the one doing the believing. If it seems to someone that the evidence for atheism is recognizably stronger than the evidence for theism, then it is reasonable for her to be an atheist. One who is a theist can try to get her to see the evidence differently. He may both try to show that her reasons for atheism are weaker than she thinks and that there are other, stronger reasons for theism. As a result, she may change her mind about the relative strength of the evidence. It may also be the case that the evidence for atheism will seem, to the atheist, stronger after she engages the theist's best efforts.

If an atheist cannot persuade a theist that the evidence for atheism is stronger than the evidence for theism, it does not follow that she is not reasonable to continue to believe that no God exists. There is a distinction between being justified and showing that one is justified in holding a belief.[6] Showing that one is justified or persuading another that one is justified in holding a belief is more difficult than knowing for oneself that one is justified in holding the belief. It is possible for a person to have evidence for atheism that seems to be recognizably stronger than the evidence for theism even if she cannot persuade someone else that the evidence actually is as strong as she thinks it is.

A nonreligious example might be helpful. Suppose a robbery occurred at noon on Saturday. Someone who looks a lot like me entered a bank and got away with a lot of money. The pictures from the security camera look like me. Witnesses identify me as the person. I know, however, that I was at home reading all day Saturday. I have no witnesses to that fact. We can make the scenario as complicated as we like. We can say that I received an anonymous gift of ten thousand dollars the same weekend. Maybe the robber even made some philosophical comment to the teller. The evidence for my guilt is, to everyone in the investigation, recognizably stronger than the evidence for my innocence. I know, however, that I am innocent. The evidence to me is certain. I was in my living room reading Christopher Hitchens the whole time. Should the strength of the evidence that is available to the police and to the witnesses undermine my own confidence in my own innocence? Should I begin to wonder whether I am really guilty? No, I should not. I might not be able to show that the evidence points to the wrong person, but I know that it does.

One other clarification is important. There are numerous positions that could be considered in the quest for a theory of ultimate reality. There are many incompatible positions that fall under the atheist rubric (and many that fall under theism, as well). Marxism and the atheism of Dawkins, for example, have very different stories about the fundamental causal processes that are at work in the world. Christian theism is different in significant ways than Islamic theism. In addition, there are alternatives that do not count as versions either of theism or of atheism. Examples include deism, pantheism, polytheism, and panentheism. This plurality of positions provides Dennett with one of his favorite arguments against God's existence. This argument will be discussed in chapter 6. In light of this range of possibilities, we can propose that for a person to be reasonable in holding any particular view, the evidence for that position has to be recognizably stronger to him than it is for any other competing position.

Mystery, Incomprehensibility, and Conflict: Faith Seeking Understanding

Dennett is concerned that something about the content of religious belief raises a special problem for the relation between faith and reason:

> In religion, however, the experts are not exaggerating for effect when they say they don't understand what they are talking about. The fundamental incomprehensibility of God is insisted upon as a central tenet of faith, and the propositions in question are themselves declared to be systematically elusive to everybody. Although we can go along with the experts when they advise us which sentences to say we believe, they also insist that *they themselves* cannot use their expertise to prove—even to one another—that they know what they are talking about. These matters are mysterious to *everybody*, experts and laypeople alike. (220; emphasis in original)

Religions do tend to hold that God is in some sense incomprehensible. This fact raises a challenge to those who would think their religion is reasonable. Can there be a reasonable belief in a being that is incomprehensible? To tackle this issue, we must first remember that most theistic religions do not teach that everything about God is incomprehensible. Most theistic religions teach that God is knowable, and that he has revealed true things about himself to human beings in ways we can understand. God is not completely comprehensible, but he is knowable. There are many elements of God's nature that we can grasp because of their connections to things we comprehend in other contexts. For example, God is taken to be a person. He has intellect and moral goodness, and he performs actions for reasons. These fundamental elements of the divine nature are within the grasp of human beings. We know about persons, about intellect and morality, and about actions from our interactions with other human persons who know and act and make moral judgments. These features about God are not incomprehensible.

It is true that it is not possible to comprehend the entire extent of God's knowledge or love, for example. This incomprehensibility, however, is no limit to the reasonableness of belief in God. A rough analogy may help. Think again of a crime. Suppose a series of calculated murders has been committed. The detectives and forensic team may gather enough evidence to point with clarity to one suspect. This evidence might be strong enough to convict the person of the crime beyond a reasonable doubt. Despite the strength of this evidence, there are many elements of the case that may seem incomprehensible. For example, despite the fact that the investigators have revealed a motive, it is still difficult to see how a person can plan and carry out such a series of brutal actions. Even our best psychological theories may not help us comprehend this kind of action. In a case like this one, we can have a combination of strong evidence to identify the person and motives and a deep inability to comprehend how those motives would be sufficient to move a human being to act brutally. Similarly, it is possible that there could be strong evidence for the existence of God even if elements of his nature remain outside our ability to comprehend them.

Navigating Conflicts between Faith and Reason

There is another important aspect of the role of reason in religious believing. Throughout history, and in the lives of most religious believers, conflicts have arisen between what a religion may ask its followers to believe and what reason seems to ask of them. If the religious believer is to defend the notion that her believing is reasonable, she needs to be able to navigate such conflicts. It is not enough to navigate them comfortably; she must navigate them in a manner that is itself reasonable. To begin to shed light on this issue, it will help to think briefly about how theists have related faith and reason throughout history.

Augustine of Hippo was concerned greatly about the relation between faith and reason. His belief that Christianity appealed to faith at the expense of reason prevented him from becoming a Christian for many years. He followed the Manichaeans because, among other things, they promised to appeal only to reason. Soon Augustine became disillusioned with this claim. The Manichaeans too appealed to faith, and, when they did appeal to evidence, their appeals often were demonstrably false. Augustine began to see the necessity of belief as well as of reason. One of his early works, *On the Usefulness of Belief*, takes up this theme.[7]

In this work, Augustine argues that both faith and reason are needed in every kind of knowledge. Faith, at least in the form of making particular assumptions that are not yet justified, cannot be dispensed with. We must assume that our senses are reliable if we are to learn anything empirically. That they are reliable is not itself a claim that can be tested empirically. We must also assume that logic is truth conducive even as we apply it to other questions. There is a kind of faith, then, that is indispensible in all kinds of knowledge.

Reason too was seen to be indispensible. When we think about believing something based on authority, whether it is the Scriptures or the academic community, we must evaluate whether the authority is reliable. We do not simply take every purported authority to be so. In this way, both faith and reason play a role in our knowledge of the world. Augustine was the first major thinker to propose the posture of *faith seeking understanding* as the right way to work out the relationship between these differing sources of knowledge.

Anselm of Canterbury is most famous for discovering the ontological argument for God's existence that we will discuss in the next chapter. His second-greatest contribution is probably the clearest development of faith seeking understanding in medieval philosophy. In the *Proslogion*, Anselm writes, "For I do not seek to understand so that I may believe; but I believe so that I may understand. For I believe this also, that 'unless I believe, I shall not understand.'"[8]

For Augustine and Anselm, both reason and faith were means to knowledge. Faith was thought of as believing in the deliverances of a reliable authority. If a reliable authority made a claim, it was reasonable to believe the claim. The opposition of faith to understanding was not that of opinion to knowledge. Augustine and Anselm thought they knew things by means of faith on the basis of the authority of the Scriptures or the Church. They sought to understand these things on the basis of reason. In this way their knowledge by means of faith would become knowledge by means of understanding as well. Authority as the basis for knowledge would be supplemented with reason as a basis for knowledge. Neither Augustine nor Anselm thought that faith generates only opinions or that one should take a merely hypothetical stance concerning the deliverances of authority until they pass the muster of reason.

It takes the application of reason to help sort out whether a purported authority is a reliable one or not. Augustine and Anselm recognized that most of the things we know are based on our believing authorities that we deem reliable. Harris agrees: "In fact, the more educated we become, the more our beliefs come to us at second hand. A person who believes only those propositions for which he can provide full sensory or theoretical justification will know almost nothing about the world; that is, if he is not swiftly killed by his own ignorance" (73). The fact that most of what we know is on the basis of secondhand information, however, does not give us license to believe any purported authority without critical reflection. We have to determine that the authority is reliable.

Once the source of authority has been recognized as reliable, the posture of faith seeking understanding can help a thoughtful believer navigate potential conflicts between faith and reason. It might be fruitful to show how such navigation might work. There are three kinds of cases. The first case is one in which a person can solve the apparent conflict directly. Augustine thought his treatment of the problem of reconciling divine foreknowledge and human freedom was a pertinent example of this case. He thought that he had achieved understanding so that he not only believed that we were free and morally responsible, as well as that God knows each of our future free choices, but that he could see how both of these claims could be true.[9]

There are cases, however, in which a scholar cannot reach understanding by reason. At this point, the religious thinker goes back to the authority and tries to determine whether the authority was truly reliable or if she had understood the teachings of the authority properly. Perhaps she had brought into the discussion assumptions that were not essential to her faith. The most famous example of this sort of case is the dispute over the heliocentric solar system.

Scholars during the time of Copernicus interpreted the Scriptures along Aristotelian lines. They thought that it was the Scriptures that taught that the earth was the center of the universe. Once enough data were brought forth to show that the earth was not the center of the universe, they encountered a conflict. Many persecuted those who spread the new doctrines because they thought there was clear teaching in the Scriptures to support the contrary. Others began to see that it was not biblical teaching but Aristotle's views that were being contradicted by Copernicus and Galileo. These scholars allowed what they learned from the new sciences to challenge the standard, Aristotelian interpretations of Scripture. When they discovered that Scripture could be and, in fact, should be interpreted as consistent with Copernican theory without compromising its authority and inspiration, they changed their position. In other words, the findings of science challenged the interpretation of the biblical authority. Science did not overthrow that authority. In this way these scholars continued to operate under the method of faith seeking understanding.

The third sort of case is the one least likely to be acceptable to the New Atheists. Sometimes a scholar will go back to the sources of authority and determine that she cannot reinterpret the authority to accommodate what it seems that reason delivers. In this case, the scholar has to determine whether this scenario undermines the religious authority or whether it is more reasonable to continue to believe what is difficult to reconcile with what reason seems to require. Perhaps it will become clear that reason does not require what we thought it did.

A historical example of this kind of case is the early disputes on the nature of Christ. The teaching of Scripture seemed to require that Jesus was both fully human and also fully God. Why did mainstream Christianity accept this position? It is not that there were no alternative interpretations on the market. Indeed, they were legion. It is as if each alternative failed the test of being consistent with what was found in the authoritative Scriptures. So, one could develop a position that satisfied the immediate demands of the understanding only by stepping outside of the bounds of established and reliable authority. Christian thinkers adopted the posture of faith seeking understanding and engaged in a long and vigorous project of working through the issues. In the end, they affirmed the dual nature of Christ.

In the case of the Copernican Revolution, the traditional interpretation of the authorities could be rejected without compromising the authority of the Scriptures. In the case of the nature of Christ, the traditional or received interpretation could not be so revised. Scholars remained in the posture of faith seeking to find understanding, although understanding was not forthcoming. This latter position can be seen to be reasonable. It must be remembered that if God exists, we ought to expect that there will be things about his nature and purposes that we will not be able to discern. They will be beyond our ability to figure them out. We often expect it to be difficult to discern another person's motives and inner thoughts. So too we ought to expect that God's reasons for acting will not always be discernible to finite human beings. Furthermore, aspects of his divine nature, especially those aspects that are least similar to the nature of finite creatures. will likely be beyond our ability to comprehend fully. This expectation is reasonable. In fact, it would be unreasonable to expect that we ought to be able to grasp fully everything about God's nature and purposes.

The charge that religions are suspect because of the role faith plays within them does not have, in the end, much to commend it. It is possible, to be sure, to hold religious beliefs in a way that is in conflict with reason. Any theoretical position, atheism included, can be held in an unreasonable way. Believing that God exists can be reasonable for a person if she has the right sort of evidence for the claim. When a religious person believes in God, she might be going beyond the mere belief that he exists. This posture includes personal commitment and trust. This commitment too can be rational if it is based on good reason to think that God exists. In this chapter, we did not discuss any reasons to think that God does exist (or that he does not). We have tried to get clear the role of faith and the role of evidence, and to show that religious faith is not incompatible with reason. In fact, as the history of theology and philosophy shows, it is worked out best in the context of thoughtful reflection.

CHAPTER THREE

Three Arguments for God

In the last chapter, we discussed the role of evidence in reasonable belief. In this chapter, we shall turn our attention to how the New Atheists interact with the sort of evidence that has been brought forward for the existence of God. This task will take us into the traditional arguments for God's existence and, specifically, the challenges that the New Atheists raise to these arguments. It is important to keep clear that our posture will be defensive rather than offensive. No case shall be attempted to show that it is, overall, reasonable to believe in God or that it is more reasonable to believe than not. Rather, it shall be argued that the criticisms leveled at arguments for God's existence are, for the most part, unsuccessful. As a result, these arguments may still provide good reason to think that God exists. In addition, we will not attempt to rebut every possible objection to these arguments. Even if they survive the criticisms of the New Atheists, there may be other considerations that count against the arguments. Our conclusion, then, will be that the work of these writers, at least, does not undermine the case for God's existence.

As we saw in discussing faith and reason, both Harris and Hitchens think there is little possibility of good evidence for the existence of God. It is not surprising, then, that they invest the least space in interacting with traditional arguments. Harris discusses the notion that religion is necessary to ground our moral lives. Hitchens dedicates an entire chapter to the design argument in the traditional form as put forward by William Paley. The rise of Darwinian theory, he thinks, shows that there is no need to appeal to design in order to explain the origin of the items Paley investigated. The complexity of the eye, for example, can be given a perfectly naturalistic explanation.

Dennett discusses the connection of religion to morality in some detail, although in *Breaking the Spell*, he spends little time on the other traditional arguments. Dennett refers readers to two of the chapters from his book *Darwin's Dangerous Idea*,[1] where he "covered these arguments quite extensively" (243). He is not optimistic about the possibility that these arguments add anything to the case for God. He explains that "I decided some time ago that diminishing returns had set in on the arguments about God's existence, and I doubt that any breakthroughs are in the offing, from either side" (27).

Dawkins addresses most of the traditional arguments in more detail than the other New Atheists. He too thinks that the arguments do not amount to support for the existence of God. Most theistic arguments aim to show that God is necessary to explain the origin or nature of something else, either the universe, or human beings, or moral reality. Dawkins thinks that these kinds of arguments fall to the simple question of the origin of God. He comments that a "designer God cannot be used to explain organized complexity because any God capable of designing anything would have to be complex enough to demand the same kind of explanation in his own right. God presents an infinite regress from which he cannot help us to escape" (109).

In this chapter, we will engage with the New Atheists' criticisms of three of the arguments they discuss. In particular, we will address their criticisms of the cosmological arguments, the ontological arguments, and the moral arguments for God's existence.

In the next chapter we will consider in greater detail their criticisms of design arguments.

Cosmological Arguments

There are two steps in most arguments for the existence of God. The first step is to argue for some kind of supernatural being. This step requires an argument that some item in the natural universe requires a supernatural cause or explanation. The second step is to argue that this supernatural being has the characteristics that are attributed to God. For the past few centuries, most of the philosophical attention has been directed at the first step in the argument. Far less energy has been spent on showing that the first cause was the God of religion.

Cosmological arguments begin with the existence of the universe and argue that it must have a cause or an explanation outside of it. If the cause or the explanation is not part of the natural universe, then it is supernatural. Like most arguments for God's existence, indeed, like most arguments in philosophy, there are a variety of versions that have been defended throughout the centuries. The most famous of the cosmological arguments are those put forward by Thomas Aquinas. In the *Summa Theologicae*, he claims that the existence of God can be proven in five ways.[2] The first three of these ways constitute cosmological arguments. Aquinas' five ways were a product of his application of Aristotle's four causes, or four means of rational explanation, to the universe itself.[3] Aristotle had argued that there were four different types of cause or explanation. A complete explanation for anything had to include its material cause, its formal cause, its efficient cause, and its final cause. It is perhaps easier to describe the differences in these causes by means of an example.

Suppose we are looking for a full explanation for a ceramic coffee mug. Why is the mug the way it is? Our answer will employ each kind of explanation. First there is the *material cause*. Part of a good and complete answer to this question involves the material out of which it is made. It is ceramic. The material out of which it is made explains a lot. It explains the fact that it is the right kind of stuff to hold together into the shape necessary to hold coffee. It explains why it is microwaveable, as well. Second, there is the *formal cause*. The formal cause is the shape or the structure of the thing that makes it what it is. For physical objects, it is often the literal shape. This item is a mug in virtue of its shape. If we were to flatten it somehow, it would no longer be a mug. Third, there is the *efficient cause*. The efficient cause is what puts the form into the matter. In this case it is some person or group of persons in a factory in China. Sometimes the efficient cause is not some person but some other object. For example, the efficient cause of the stain on the ceiling in my house is the water that is even now leaking into it through the hole in the roof. It is tempting to think that Aristotle's efficient cause captures what we usually mean by a cause. The efficient cause for Aristotle, however, is never an event; it is always a substance. Fourth, there is the *final cause*. The final cause is perhaps the most puzzling. The final cause is the end or goal toward which, or for which, the object is made or functions. It is easy, on the one hand, to see how the purpose for which some artifact is made is an important part of a complete explanation of the artifact. This mug was made in order to hold coffee so I can take a sip. Talking about final causation in natural things as opposed to artifacts is more controversial. Aristotle would say that the final cause for a living thing is its flourishing in the unique functions that characterize the kind of living thing it is.

Each of Aquinas' five ways to prove the existence of God is the application of one of Aristotle's four causes. The first two ways each apply the notion of efficient cause. First, Aquinas looks for the efficient cause of motion. (Motion, for Aquinas as for Aristotle, included all kinds of alteration, not simply a change in spatial location.) Second, he looks for the efficient cause of existence. Aquinas argues, in each case, that nothing can be the efficient cause of its own motion or its own existence. If this is the case, then either there is an infinite regress of efficient causes of motion or of existence or there is a first efficient cause that was not caused by something else. The most important part of Aquinas' arguments is his attempt to show that the infinite regress is not possible.

Neither Aquinas nor Aristotle thought that infinite causal regresses in general were impossible. Only certain kinds of regresses could not go on to infinity. A causal regress in which each element stands in transitive relations to the others, they thought, could not be infinite. This kind of regress was described by Aquinas and other medieval Aristotelians as a series that is ordered per se. A transitive regress that is not causal can be infinite. For example, the "greater than" relation is transitive. In arithmetic, it is infinite. For every number, there is a higher number. A regress or series that is both transitive and causal cannot be infinite.

A causal regress that is not transitive also can be infinite. This kind of regress is ordered *per accidens.* An example might help. Suppose John is the father of William, and William is the father of Stephen. The being-father-of relation, Aquinas thinks, is a causal regress that can go on to infinity because it is not transitive. In the case of John, William, and Stephen, we would not say that John is the father of Stephen. What John causes, so to speak, is the birth of William. The birth of William is not what causes the birth of Stephen, however. So the parental relation is not ordered per se. It is ordered *per accidens.*

Why is it that a transitive causal series (ordered per se) cannot be infinite? Suppose there is a chain attached to a car that is towing a trailer. The first link in the chain causes the second link to move. The second link causes the third to move, and so on. This relation is ordered per se because what the motion of the first link causes is the motion of the second link. The motion of the second link is the very thing that causes the motion of the third link. If we try to explain the motion of the third link of the chain, we do not need to appeal to the motion of the second link. We can explain it in virtue of the motion of the first link or the motion of the car. The middle link, in a sense, drops out of the explanation of the motion of the chain (or of the trailer). It turns out that we can explain the motion of the trailer without appeal to the motion of the chain at all. The car, we say, tows the trailer. Suppose there were no "first link." In other words, there was no car, but the chain was of infinite length. We would not be able to explain the motion of the chain or the trailer at all. Each link in the chain drops out of the explanation. In order to have an explanation for the motion of the trailer, then, the chain must be finite. This illustration captures what sort of causal regress Aquinas thought had to be finite. A chain of efficient causes of motion was the kind of regress that could not go on to infinity. Therefore, there must be a first efficient cause of motion that is not itself moved by anything else.

Each of Aquinas' arguments is structured similarly. His second way appeals to a series of efficient causes for existence. This series too is ordered per se and cannot be infinite. There must be a first cause, not only of motion or change but of existence. The third way is an argument from material cause. He thought that contingent things have the seeds of their own dissolution within them. Therefore, there cannot be an infinite series of contingent things. His fourth and fifth ways treat the formal and final causes respectively.[4]

The next most important form of the cosmological argument is related to Aquinas' third way. This is the argument of Samuel Clarke and Gottfried Wilhelm Leibniz. Clarke and Leibniz, though they disagreed about many things, each offered an argument for the existence of God based on the *principle of sufficient reason*.[5] The principle of sufficient reason is the principle that every fact or truth is such that there is a sufficient reason for its being a fact or being true.

Cosmological arguments of this kind begin with the fact that the universe exists and that it is contingent. Because it is contingent, it did not have to exist. It could have been the case that the universe failed to exist. The principle of sufficient reason requires that there be a sufficient reason for the existence of the universe. Either this reason is found within the universe or it is found outside the universe. If it is found within the universe, then the universe itself contains the reason for its existence. If this were the case, the universe would be necessary and not contingent. There-fore the reason for the universe must lie outside of it.

Whatever counts as the sufficient reason for the universe must also have a sufficient reason for its existence. There will either be an infinite series of contingent entities, each of which explains the next, or the series will end in a necessarily existing being that is the sufficient reason for its own existence as well as for the exis-tence of the entire series. Clarke and Leibniz think that an infinite series of contingent things is not sufficient to explain its own exis-tence, even if each item in the series has an explanation. There also needs to be an explanation for the series itself. Therefore, there must exist a necessarily existing being that is the sufficient reason for the existence of everything else.

Although this argument has proven to be influential and per-suasive to many, it suffers a devastating flaw. The principle of suf-ficient reason turns out to be false. It is not the case that for every fact or truth there is a sufficient reason for its reality or truth. Peter van Inwagen has argued that if the principle of sufficient reason is true, then there are no contingent truths. Since there are contingent truths, the principle must be false.

Suppose all of the contingent truths in the universe are con-joined into one long sentence. This sentence is itself a contingent truth. If the principle of sufficient reason is true, then there is a sufficient reason for this truth. That reason must be a necessary truth (since all contingent truths are within the sentence). Thus far, his argument parallels the cosmological arguments of Leib-niz and Clarke. Van Inwagen goes on to argue that if x is a suf-ficient reason for y, then x entails y. That is if x is true, y must be true. The important point is that if x entails y, and x is necessary, then y is also necessary. So if there is a sufficient reason for the sentence that is a conjunction of all contingent truths, and that reason is itself necessary, then the sentence consisting of all con-tingent truths turns out to be necessary. Since it is supposed that all contingent truths are contained within this sentence, it turns out that there are no contingent truths.[6] But it seems obvious that there are contingent truths. For example, the fact that there was an even number of mosquitoes in Connecticut at noon on August 11, 2008, appears to be a contingent truth. The number could have been odd. If the principle of sufficient reason is true, then this number is necessary. It could not have been otherwise. If van Inwagen is right, and the principle of sufficient reason is false, then this version of the cosmological argument is not sound.

A third form of the cosmological argument that has enjoyed a resurgence of interest in recent times is called the *kalam cosmological argument.*[7] The kalam argument is so named after the medieval Islamic movement of scholasticism in which it originated. The kalam cosmological argument aims to show that, since everything that comes into existence is caused to exist by something outside it, and the universe came into existence, the universe was caused to exist by something outside it. The distinctive feature of the kalam argument is how the claim that the universe came into existence is defended. There are two lines of support. First, it is argued that an infinite collection of anything is simply impossible. If the past is infinite, then the collection of past events is an infinite collection. If it is impossible for there to be an infinite collection of anything, then the collection of past events must be finite. Therefore, the universe must have a finite past.

The second support for the claim that the universe came into existence is that it is impossible to complete any infinite series by successive addition. This claim can be shown to be plausible by considering why it is impossible to count to infinity. No matter how long one counts, one reaches only finite numbers. Counting to infinity is an example of attempting to complete an infinite series by successive addition. The past is a series of moments (or years, or days) that was formed in succession, one at a time. Furthermore, the past is complete. Tomorrow is not part of the past, although it will be part of it. If the past is infinite, then it is an infinite series. Therefore, there would be an infinite series that was completed by successive addition. If the past is infinite, then an infinite number of years has passed, one at a time. If an infinite number of years has passed, then we should never have reached today. It took an infinite number of years to reach this day; but it also took an infinite number of years to reach any other date in the past. For example, to reach the origin of the universe twenty billion years ago took exactly as long as it took to reach today. The puzzle shows that an infinite series cannot be completed by successive addition. If the kalam argument supports the impossibility of an infinite past, then the universe came into existence. Therefore, it was caused to exist by something outside it. Therefore, there is a supernatural first cause.

Each of these kinds of cosmological argument has generated significant ongoing discussion. Both Dawkins and Dennett offer criticisms of the cosmological argument, although Dennett confines his to one paragraph:

> The Cosmological Argument, which in its simplest form states that since everything must have a cause the universe must have a cause—namely, God—doesn't stay simple for long. Some deny the premise, since quantum physics teaches us (doesn't it?) that not everything that happens needs to have a cause. Others prefer to accept the premise and then ask: What caused God? The reply that God is self-caused (somehow) raises the rebuttal: If something can be self-caused, why can't the universe as a whole be the thing that is self-caused? This leads in various arcane directions, into the strange precincts of string theory and probability fluctuations and the like, at one extreme, and into ingenious nitpicking about the meaning of "cause" at the other. Unless you have a taste for mathematics and theoretical physics on the one hand, or the niceties of scholastic logic on the other, you are not apt to find any of this compelling, or even fathomable. (242)

Dennett's major objection seems to be a concern that an argument that can be stated very simply, in its most basic form, becomes very complicated. This kind of complicating process helps to fuel the impatience that many people have with philosophy—and with scholarship in general. Unfortunately, the academic enterprise is fraught with these kinds of complications. As soon as a simple argument is presented, objections can be raised. Each objection requires a response that makes the kind of distinctions that either modify the original argument or attempt to show that the objection does not count against the basic structure of the argument. This move, in turn, results in more objections. It is easy to see how any theory, whether a philosophical argument or a scientific hypothesis, can become so complicated as to lose the interest of the majority of people. That discussion of the cosmological argument will become complicated is not a cogent criticism of the argument.

His next concern is that the argument leaves open the question of the cause of God. This objection is expressed often in the pages of both Dennett's and Dawkins' books. We shall address it as a general challenge in chapter 6. Here we should consider whether the cosmological argument in particular leaves the theist open to this objection. The way that Dennett summarizes the argument certainly leaves it vulnerable to this objection. If everything must have a cause, then God must have a cause as well. No historically important version of the argument, however, claims that everything must have a cause. The argument is always articulated in such a way that *some* things need causes. For example, Aquinas' first way argues that changing things (what he calls, following Aristotle, things in motion) require a cause for their change. Since Aquinas argues that God does not change, God does not require a cause according to this argument. The kalam argument and Aquinas' second way endorse the claim that everything that comes into existence needs to be caused to exist by something outside of it. If there are eternal things, that is, things that never come into existence from nonexistence, they do not require a cause. This argument also does not require that God needs a cause. If there are other things that are eternal, such as mathematical truths or abstract objects, these too are immune from this premise of the argument. The Leibniz-Clarke kind of argument and Aquinas' third way claim that contingent things require an explanation outside of themselves. God does not require an explanation outside of himself because he is a necessarily existing being. The structure of the various cosmological arguments does not leave them open to Dennett's criticisms. Dennett stops short after his first, brief objection. As a result, he does not interact accurately with any of the significant versions of the cosmological argument.

Dawkins raises some of the same criticisms of the cosmological arguments that Dennett has raised. He argues, as we saw, that these arguments "rely upon the idea of a regress and invoke God to terminate it. They make the entirely unwarranted assumption that God himself is immune to the regress" (77). Rather than invoking God to terminate a regress, Dawkins suggests that "it is more parsimonious to conjure up, say, a 'big bang singularity,' or some other physical concept as yet unknown" (78). He points out, further, that there are regresses that reach a termination without appeal to God. His example is that we can continue to cut a piece of gold into smaller and smaller pieces. After every cut, what is left is still gold. This regress ends when we get to the molecular level. Eventually, the small piece of gold left is one atom. We can cut that up, but what will remain will no longer be gold. So some regresses have natural terminations and others are such that not even God can terminate them.

Dawkins is correct about both of these claims. Not every regress requires a supernatural termination, and there are regresses that even God cannot terminate. As we saw, Dennett suggested a version of the cosmological argument that is based on one such regress. These two facts, however, do not count against the cosmological argument. What Dawkins must show is that the argument as offered employs a regress that either cannot be terminated by God or can be terminated by some other natural thing. He has offered no reason to think the particular regresses employed fall into these categories. In fact, in each case, it is at least plausible both that natural things cannot terminate the regress and that God can.

Dawkins' suggestion that it is more parsimonious to suggest that some physical item is the termination of these regresses is a case in point. Aquinas' first way invokes a regress of changes. Since physical things are subject to change, no physical thing can terminate that regress. Nor can the big bang singularity terminate the regress of causes of existence. To argue, as some have done, that the big bang singularity is a brute fact is not to suggest a naturalistic version of the unmoved mover. It is to hold that things can pop into existence without any cause at all. Dennett's reference to quantum events above is relevant here. Quantum events appear to be things that pop into existence without a cause. One who would defend Aquinas' second way and the kalam argument would have to argue that the origin of the universe is not sufficiently similar to a quantum event to overrule the widely established principle that, at least in general, things do not come into existence without a cause.

Because physical things are contingently existing things, they cannot terminate the regress in the Leibniz-Clarke-type argument. That the big bang singularity as the terminus of the regress might be more parsimonious is relevant only if it can successfully terminate the regress. Since it cannot, these criticisms fall wide of the mark.

Dawkins' second criticism of the cosmological argument is that "there is absolutely no reason to endow that terminator [of the regress] with any of the properties normally ascribed to God . . ." (77). Dawkins is right that the cosmological argument as articulated does not provide a reason to think that the terminator of the regress has all of the features normally thought to be true of God. As we saw, the reason for this lack is that these arguments are the first step of the two-step argument for God's existence. Once it is granted that there is an unmoved mover, or a necessarily existing thing that is the sufficient reason for the existence of the universe, it takes further argumentation to support the idea that this being is God as traditionally conceived.

It is not hard to begin to sketch briefly how such an argument would go. For example, the first cause must have more power than anything within the universe. Second, the first cause is not physical. Third, it can even be argued that it must be a person who acts for reasons. This last claim can be supported based on the fact that all of the necessary and sufficient conditions for the triggering of the big bang were available eternally. The universe, however, is only about twenty billion years old. Why is it not older? The only kind of cause we know about that triggers an event when all of the other necessary and sufficient conditions are already present is the will of a personal agent. These lines of thought are meant only to suggest that the task of arguing from the existence of, say, a first cause to a being something like the traditional notion of God is not too difficult. It ought to be noted that Aquinas devoted several hundred pages to developing many arguments that the first cause is God.

In summary, the cosmological arguments for God's existence are immune from most of the published criticisms of the New Atheists. To be sure, one who supports Aquinas' version or the kalam version has to revise the principle that whatever comes into existence is caused to exist by something else. Quantum events serve as counterexamples to this principle. The revised argument will be short of a proof. It seems impossible to rule out the possibility that the universe popped into existence with absolutely no cause. Rather than claiming that everything that comes into existence is caused to exist by something else, the modified argument will claim that it is highly likely that something like the universe would not come into existence without a cause. Such an argument, if successful, would still be a strong argument, though not a proof, that God exists.

Ontological Arguments

The ontological argument for God's existence is unique among theistic arguments in that it does not begin with some item or fact in the natural world. Rather it begins with the concept of God. The argument was discovered by Anselm of Canterbury, though it may have been anticipated by the Islamic philosopher Ibn Sina (Avicenna), who lived between 980 and 1037. It is highly likely, however, that Anselm's discovery of the argument was independent of Ibn Sina's work. The ontological argument has fascinated philosophers ever since. Several versions were offered and criticized throughout the history of philosophy. Theistic arguments such as the cosmological, moral, and design arguments, even though they can be technical, connect with hunches that are widely shared by nonphilosophers. It is hard to imagine someone coming to believe in God because they had a hunch that reflected the ontological argument.

In the *Proslogion*, which is written as a prayer, Anselm states the argument:

> Now we believe that You are something than which nothing greater can be thought. Or can it be that a thing of such a nature does not exist, since "the Fool has said in his heart, there is no God" [Ps 13:1, 52:1]? But surely, when this same Fool hears what I am speaking about, namely, "something-than-which-nothing-greater-can-be-thought," he understands what he hears, and what he understands is in his mind, even if he does not understand that it actually exists. For it is one thing for an object to exist in the mind, and another thing to understand that an object actually exists . . . . For if it exists solely in the mind, it can be thought to exist in reality also, which is greater. If then that-than-which-a-greater-cannot-be-thought exists in the mind alone, this same that-than-which-a-greater-*cannot*-be-thought is that-than-which-a-greater-*can*-be-thought. But this is obviously impossible. Therefore there is absolutely no doubt that something-than-which-a-greater-cannot-be-thought exists both in the mind and in reality.[8]

The concept of God includes the notion that God is the greatest possible being. If we imagine that God does not exist, then we are imagining the greatest possible being not existing. But, so the argument goes, then we can imagine an even greater being. We can imagine a God who does exist. So the greatest possible being that does not exist in actuality would not be the greatest possible being. It must be the case, therefore, that the greatest possible being exists in reality and not just in our imagination.

Contemporary discussion of this argument usually attributes a devastating criticism to Immanuel Kant:

> *Being* is obviously not a real predicate, i.e., a concept of something that could add to the concept of a thing. It is merely the positing of a thing or of certain determinations in themselves. In

the logical use it is merely the copula of a judgment. The proposition *God is omnipotent* contains two concepts that have their objects: God and omnipotence; the little word "*is*" is not a predicate in it, but only that which posits the predicate *in relation* to the subject. Now if I take the subject (God) together with all his predicates (among which omnipotence belongs), and say *God is*, or there is a God, then I add no new predicate to the concept of God, but only posit the subject in itself with all its predicates, and indeed posit the *object* in relation to my *concept*[9]

The objection that the ontological argument assumes, falsely, that existence is a predicate or a property is not original with Kant, however. Pierre Gassendi raises the same challenge to Descartes in his objections to the ontological argument Descartes offered in his *Meditations*. Gassendi claims,

In fact, however, existence is not a perfection either in God or in anything else; it is that without which no perfections can be present. For surely, what does not exist has no perfections or imperfections, and what does exist and has several perfections does not have existence as one of its individual perfections; rather, its existence is that in virtue of which both the thing itself and its perfections are existent.[10]

Existence is not one quality a thing can have, along with its size, color, and location. Rather, it is what is presupposed for any object if that object is to have other properties. Anselm's argument, that imagining God not existing is imagining a being with all of the properties of God except existence, is flawed.

Descartes' response to Gassendi is instructive. He first tries to defend the notion that existence is a perfection, but he quickly gives this up:

Here I do not see what sort of thing you want existence to be, nor why it cannot be said to be a property just like omnipotence—provided, of course, that we take the word "property" to stand for any attribute, or for whatever can be predicated of a thing; and this is exactly how it should be taken in this context. Moreover, in the case of God necessary existence is in fact a property in the strictest sense of the term, since it applies to him alone and forms a part of his essence as it does of no other thing.[11]

Although Descartes thinks that existence ought to be counted as a property in the broad sense, he realize that he does not need it to be a property in order to have a sound ontological argument. All he needs is for necessary existence to be a property. And, of course, it is a property.[12]

The strongest version of the ontological argument, then, will not require existence to be a property. Rather, it will hold that a being than-which-none-greater-can-be-conceived will have necessary existence. This move is plausible in that one can compare two existing items that have similar properties. If one of them is such that, beyond existing in actuality, it also cannot fail to exist, it is reasonable to think that it is metaphysically greater than the first item. That some being exists necessarily adds to its greatness in a way that existence might not.

The ontological argument often strikes one as being some kind of trick. Dawkins refers to it as "infantile" (80) and as a "mere word game" (81). He expresses disappointment and wonder that philosophers such as Bertrand Russell and J. L. Mackie wrestled with it seriously. Dawkins' more important objections are better expressed by Dennett, so it is on Dennett's discussion that we will focus. Dennett mentions four objections. First, he asks, "Do you find this compelling? Or do you suspect that it is some sort of logical 'trick with mirrors'?" (241). Dennett is tapping into a hunch that many thinkers have had when confronting the argument. It does seem to be a trick. Of course, to criticize the argument requires showing exactly how it is a trick.

Second, Dennett raises the concern that dates back to one of Anselm's own contemporaries, that it is possible to use the kind of reasoning employed in the ontological argument to prove the existence of anything. His example is the most perfect ice cream sundae conceivable. (Gaunilo used the example of the perfect island.[13]) The concept of a most perfect ice cream sundae includes actual existence (and necessary existence). Therefore, it must exist!

This objection raises an important point. First of all, what is it that makes one being greater than another? The comparison is metaphysical. One being is greater than another if it has "great-making properties" that the other lacks or if it has those properties to a greater extent than the other being does.[14] A being than-which-none-greater-can-be-conceived will have every great- making property to the greatest possible extent. It is plausible to include things like maximal power, maximal knowledge, consciousness, and maximal goodness in a list of great-making properties. To posit a greatest possible island or an ice cream sundae raises the question of what great-making properties these things would have. Alvin Plantinga suggests that these kinds of items have evaluative properties that have no intrinsic maximum. How large will the ice cream sundae be? How many cherries will it have? These properties do not seem to admit of a maximum. The properties attributed to God, in general, do. For example, maximal power is power to do any possible task. To have maximal knowledge is to have knowledge of whatever can be known. Plantinga makes this response to the perfect island objection fairly tentatively and concludes, "there may be a weak point here in Anselm's argument . . ." (*God*, 91).

We can challenge Dennett's counterexample. Is necessary existence the sort of great-making property that an ice cream sundae can have? An ice cream sundae is a physical thing. Such things are subject to the laws of nature and, as such, they are contingent. It is part of the nature of an ice cream sundae that it exists only contingently. Therefore, necessary existence cannot be a great-making property of an ice cream sundae. Dennett's parallel argument strategy, therefore, falls short of refuting the ontological argument.

Dennett, third, refers to Kant's criticism that "you can't prove the existence of *anything* (other than an abstraction) by sheer logic" (241; emphasis in original). Dennett appears to be referring to Kant's argument that the fact that existence is not a predicate results in all existence claims being synthetic:

> I ask you: is the proposition, *This or that thing* (which I have
> conceded to you as possible, whatever it may be) *exists*—is this
> proposition, I say, an analytic or a synthetic proposition? If it is
> the former, then with existence you add nothing to your thought
> of the thing; but then either the thought that is in you must be
> the thing itself, or else you have presupposed an existence as
> belonging to possibility, and then inferred that existence on this
> pretext from its inner possibility, which is nothing but a miser-
> able tautology. . . . If you concede, on the contrary, as in all fair-
> ness you must, that every existential proposition is synthetic,
> then how would you assert that the predicate of existence may
> not be cancelled without contradiction?—since this privilege
> pertains only in the analytic propositions, as resting on its very
> character. (Kant A598/B626; emphasis in original)

Kant has argued that there are three kinds of judgments.[15] Some
are analytic a priori judgments, such as those in logic. These judgments, if true, are necessarily true. In an analytic judgment the
concept of the subject includes the concept of the predicate. An
example is that "No bachelor is married." Being unmarried is contained in the concept of bachelor, and it is by analysis that we
see that this is a necessary truth. Other judgments are synthetic
a posteriori. These are the judgments we make about the world
of sense experience. For example, the judgment that there is a
book on the table is not necessary, and we must learn that it is
true from sense experience. The third form of judgment is the
synthetic a priori. These are not analytic, in that the predicate
is not contained in the subject, nor are these a posteriori. They
are not learned from experience. Examples for Kant include the
judgments of arithmetic and geometry. That the shortest distance
between two points is a straight line (Kant knew only of Euclidean
geometry) is a necessary truth but not one in which the predicate
is contained in the subject. We can analyze the concept "the shortest distance between two points" all we want and we will never
discover within it the concept "a straight line."[16]

Kant's criticism of the ontological argument in this passage
is based on the claim that only in analytic judgments are the

predicates contained in the subject. Prime examples of analytic judgments are the judgments of logic. It is here that Dennett's objection that the ontological argument is a matter of sheer logic and therefore cannot prove the existence of something plays a role. The ontological argument, Kant thinks, is built on the premise that the concept of God contains the predicate of existence. Therefore, the argument assumes that the statement that God exists is analytic. The judgment that something exists, however, is synthetic. Existence is not something that can be contained in the concept of a subject, and therefore the argument fails.

We can clarify these issues if we assume for a moment that existence is a property, even though we know it is not. It is important, on this assumption, to distinguish between having the property of existence necessarily and having the property of necessary existence. To have a property necessarily means that having that property is essential to the object. This means the object has the property in every possible world in which the object exists. It is plausible that Kant, for example, has the property of being a human being necessarily. There is no way the world could be such that Kant exists, and not be a human being. This claim does not imply that Kant exists in every possible world. It means that if Kant exists, Kant is a human being. If existence is a property, then every object has it necessarily. That is, there is no possible world in which an object exists but does not have the property of existence. The concept of every object includes existence. When the principle is stated in this way, the point is obvious. Of course, it is better not to think of existence as a property at all.

For an object to have the property of necessary existence, however, is not simply for it to exist in every possible world in which it exists. It is for it to exist in every possible world. There is no way the world could be such that the object does not exist. It is the latter that applies to God in the ontological argument, but it is the former that Kant is arguing against above. Therefore, Kant's objection does not count against this version of the ontological argument.

Dennett's last criticism is that what the ontological argument supports, if it is sound, is the existence of a being far removed from the God of religion. He describes the being that the onto-logical argument aims to prove "a remarkably bare and featureless intentional object. Even if a *Being greater than which nothing can be conceived* has to exist, as their arguments urge, it is a long haul from that specification to a Being that is merciful or just or lov-ing . . ." (242). A being with all of the great-making properties possible to a being, however, quickly begins to appear to be the God of religion. It has, as we said, maximal power and knowledge; it is conscious and has maximal goodness, among other properties. In fact, one of the reasons Anselm thought this argument was sig-nificant is that it had the resources to derive very simply all of the traditional attributes of God.

The criticisms of the ontological argument that are offered by Dawkins and Dennett are finally unsuccessful. They do endorse the historic position that existence is not a property. This objec-tion counts against Anselm's first version of the argument. The version that ascribes necessary existence as a great-making prop-erty, however, survives this challenge.

Moral Arguments

The moral argument for God's existence is possibly as popular as the design argument. Moral truth or moral reality does not seem, to many people, to fit into an atheistic universe. Dostoevsky is well known for putting the sentiment, if not the actual words, "If there is no God, everything is permitted," into the mouth of one of his most notorious characters. Popular religious writers have developed various arguments that morality points to God.[17] Their sentiments capture a widespread hunch that morality is somehow connected to religion.

In order to make any progress in thinking about the relation-ship between God and morality, it must be recognized that there are several independent questions that are involved in this discus-sion. These questions must be kept distinct if we are to engage the topics with clarity. At least three questions are paramount: First, do we need God in order to behave morally? Second, do we need God in order to know what is right and wrong? Third, is God necessary in order for there to be objective, binding moral obligations? Each of these questions raises topics that can enter into versions of arguments for the idea that morality points to God. The New Atheists focus almost all of their attention on the first two questions, though it is the third that has potential for a strong argument for the existence of God.

Do We Need God in Order to Behave Morally?

It is not surprising that Hitchens' chapter, entitled "Does Religion Make People Behave?" focuses on this first question. He marshals what amounts to an anecdotal case for the claim that religion has played mostly a negative role in terms of helping people act morally:

> Anybody, therefore, who uses the [Martin Luther] King legacy to justify the role of religion in public life must accept all the corollaries of what they seem to be implying. Even a glance at the whole record will show, first, that person for person, American freethinkers and agnostics and atheists come out the best. The chance that someone's *secular* or freethinking opinion would cause him or her to denounce the whole injustice was extremely high. The chance that someone's religious belief would cause him or her to take a stand against slavery and racism was statistically quite small. But the chance that someone's religious belief would cause him or her to uphold slavery and racism was statistically extremely *high*, and the latter fact helps us to understand why the victory of simple justice took so long to bring about. (180; emphasis in original)

The way that Hitchens frames this observation reveals that there are two issues at work here. First, his claim amounts to a significant historical generalization. Second, there is the beginning of an argument for the claim that morality is independent of religion. While it may be that Hitchens is correct about the way responses to slavery and racism tracked religious belief in the two eras of American history considered, the general claim that the more religious one is, the less likely one is to do the right thing requires much more evidence than he has provided. For one thing, he picks only two areas of morality by which to compare religious with nonreligious people. Second, what is the right thing to do will be in dispute between thinking people in many moral dilemmas (though not the ones concerning slavery and racism that Hitchens discusses). Third, it is not clear that Hitchens has supported his claim even concerning racism and slavery. It might be the case that the most visible moral failures of religious people in America are in the areas of slavery and racism. Still, to defend the broad claim that "[t]he chance that someone's religious belief would cause him or her to take a stand against slavery and racism was statistically quite small. But the chance that someone's religious belief would cause him or her to uphold slavery and racism was statistically extremely *high*" requires thorough historical and statistical research rather than anecdotal evidence or a simple assertion.

Hitchens' claim here is also an argument that we do not, in fact, need to believe in God in order to behave morally. If he turns out to be correct that being religious is more closely connected with doing the wrong thing than with doing the right thing, then the conclusion follows. Daniel Dennett provides a similar argument. First he outlines what he takes to be the way that religion is supposed to help people behave morally:

> Without the divine carrot and stick, goes this reasoning, people would loll about aimlessly or indulge their basest desires, break their promises, cheat on their spouses, neglect their duties, and so on. There are two well-known problems with this reasoning: (1) it doesn't seem to be true, which is good news, since (2) it is such a demeaning view of human nature. (279)

Dennett then connects the previous assessment with an empirical claim:

> I have uncovered no evidence to support the claim that people, religious or not, who *don't* believe in reward in heaven and/or punishment in hell are more likely to kill, rape, rob, or break their promise than people who do. (279; emphasis in original)[18]

The conclusion is that it is not necessary for a person to believe in God in order to act morally. It must be added that Dennett has challenged this claim in another way. In chapter 2 we saw that he raised the concern of "belief in belief": a person who thinks that belief in God is important whether or not it is true has belief in belief. The claim that belief in God is necessary for us to act morally can be an example of belief in belief. As Dawkins notes, "Even if it were true that we need God to be moral, it would of course not make God's existence more likely, merely more desirable (many people cannot tell the difference)" (231).

It is possible to construct an argument for God's existence based on the claim that belief in God does help people act morally. Such an argument, however, will not be strong. The New Atheists have claimed that there is little reason to think that the claim on which such an argument is based is true. It may be that it is false and that there is evidence that it is false. At least anecdotally, there are plenty of examples of atheists who are extremely moral and of theists who are not. The believer who thinks that morality in some way points to God is better off not pressing this form of the argument.

Do We Need God in Order to Know What is Right and Wrong?

The second question that is often raised about the connection between God and morality is, "Do we need God in order to know what is right and wrong?" Harris challenges this notion:

> The pervasive idea that religion is somehow the *source* of our deepest ethical intuitions is absurd. We no more get our sense that cruelty is wrong from the pages of the Bible than we get our sense that two plus two equals four from the pages of a textbook on mathematics. Anyone who does not harbor some rudimentary sense that cruelty is wrong is unlikely to learn that it is by reading. . . . (171–72; emphasis in original)

The claim that we need God to know what is right or wrong can be mapped onto a scale of positions. On one end, one could argue that all of our deepest ethical intuitions require belief in God.

This side of the scale is the one that Harris thinks is absurd. Closer to the other end of the scale, one could argue that some of the details of moral reality are such that we need for God to reveal them to us. On the first side of the scale is the claim that the very notion of a moral intuition requires God. Unless we believe in God, this position claims, our moral intuitions are not reliable guides to moral reality. Near the other side of the scale is the claim that there are at least some details of moral obligations that require some special revelation from God. This latter position is consistent with denying that religious belief is necessary to know every moral truth.

Both Dawkins and Dennett defend the notion that both our capacities for moral evaluation and at least some of the content of our moral beliefs can be given a Darwinian explanation. They argue that even altruistic behavior can be explained in this way. The fact that we will sacrifice for our children and others in our family or circle of friends, and the fact that we feel as though there is some kind of obligation to do so, they think, can be given a straightforwardly Darwinian explanation. As a result, we do not need God or to believe in God in order to know that such sacrifice is good.

It is not necessary to engage the details of their arguments for this claim because they are correct. The fact that we have a moral sense and the fact that we take altruistic behavior, for example, to be morally good behavior can be explained along Darwinian lines. As a result, the claim that we need God to make sense of the fact that we have a moral sense is not well supported. The closer one is to the first side of the "all moral knowledge depends on God" scale, the less secure one's position is.

If God exists, then our moral sense is, in some way, a product of divine design (even if the divine mechanism is broadly Darwinian in nature). It does not follow from the divine origins of our moral sense that our believing in God will make us less likely to make moral mistakes. After all, if God exists, our sense of smell has a similar divine origin. A discerning sense of smell is not something that belief in God generally improves.

In a narrow range of cases, it might be that believing in God can help our moral discernment. If God exists and has a plan for how we live, it is reasonable to think (though it does not follow of necessity) that part of this plan has to do with specifics in our moral or spiritual lives. He could give particular commands, then, that could be related to some of the aspects of his particular plan. It is possible, then, that there are some cases in which believing God's revelation has implications for our moral discernment. Apart from the small range of cases alluded to here, we can still agree with the New Atheists that the existence of God, or belief in God, is not necessary in order for us to know what is right or wrong.

Is God Necessary in Order to Have Objective, Binding Moral Obligations?

The bottom line from our discussion so far is that the New Atheists are correct about the first two questions concerning the connection between God and morality. Despite the fact that some believers may try to develop arguments based on these concerns for the claim that God exists, such arguments will not be very promising. The third question, it will be seen, is a more fruitful arena for an argument that morality, in some sense, requires the existence of God.

This kind of moral argument is based on the notion that there is something about the nature of moral obligations that makes more sense if God exists than if God does not exist. This feature of moral obligations is that they are real or objective. It is important to get clear what we mean by calling these obligations real or objective. Often people use the term *absolute* to try to capture this aspect of moral facts. To call moral obligations absolute, however, is misleading because it carries the connotation that the obligation is one for which there can be no exception. So if it is an absolute moral obligation not to tell a lie, then there can be no exceptions to this prohibition. While it might be the case that there are obligations that are absolute in this way, we would do well not to structure our argument in a way that requires there to be such obligations. It might be that there are no moral obligations that are completely immune from exception. This feature is why it can be misleading to call moral obligations absolute.

Instead, to call moral obligations *objective* is to imply that the fact that we are under the obligation is not something that is up to us. That an obligation is binding on us is not determined by the dictates of our culture or whether or not we want to obey the obligation. The binding nature of the obligation is independent of these things. Harris, for one, does not want to reject the objective nature of moral obligation. He launches a sustained attack on relativism. His own moral theory is grounded in facts concerning the suffering or happiness that can be experienced:

> A rational approach to ethics becomes possible once we real-
> ize that questions of right and wrong are really questions about
> the happiness and suffering of sentient creatures. If we are in a
> position to affect the happiness or suffering of others, we have
> ethical responsibilities toward them. (170–71)

Note that Harris thinks both that moral obligations are real and objective and that they can be grounded rationally in the facts about the possibility of sentient creatures experiencing happiness or suffering. He is well aware that the difficulty of explaining objective moral facts leads many people to reject the idea that there are such moral facts:

> Many people appear to believe that ethical truths are culturally
> contingent in a way that scientific truths are not. Indeed, this
> loss of purchase upon ethical *truth* seems to be one of the prin-
> cipal shortcomings of secularism. The problem is that once we
> abandon our belief in a rule-making God, the question of *why*
> a given action is good or bad becomes a matter of debate. And
> a statement like "Murder is wrong," while being uncontroversial
> in most circles, has never seemed anchored to the facts of this
> world in the way that statements about planets or molecules
> appear to be. The problem, in philosophical terms, has been one

of characterizing just what sort of "facts" our moral intuitions can be said to track—if, indeed, they track anything of the kind. (170; emphasis in original)

The other New Atheists are less explicit in their commitment to the objective nature of moral obligations. The fact that they make many moral arguments against religious belief, or the way religious believers have held their beliefs, however, indicates that they think there are objective obligations. Without objective moral obligations, their arguments are really expressions of their own preferences. It is far more likely that they put forward these arguments because they think there are real moral standards that have been violated.

The most promising arguments that moral reality points to God are based on the objective nature of moral obligations. We will discuss one such argument from George Mavrodes, and one that builds on some of my own previously published work. Mavrodes has argued that moral obligations do not fit well in a universe without God.[19] He develops this argument first by laying out the sketch of a nontheistic universe. He calls it the "Russellian world" after Bertrand Russell, who expressed the essence of this worldview in his essay, "A Free Man's Worship." A Russellian world is one in which "man is the product of causes which had no prevision of the end they were achieving . . ." (Mavrodes, 215, citing Russell). The Russellian world, it turns out, is very similar to the way the New Atheists believe the world is in reality. Mavrodes observes that in a Russellian world, there are certain benefits and goods that are possible. He calls these "Russellian benefits," and he gives some examples. "A contented old age would be, I suppose, a Russellian benefit, as would a thrill of sexual pleasure or a good reputation. Going to heaven when one dies, though a benefit, is not a Russellian benefit" (216).

Mavrodes then discusses the concept of morality. He takes it that morality gives rise to judgments concerning some action that some particular person in a given situation has a duty to perform or to avoid some action. Secondly, he highlights what we have been calling the objective nature of moral obligations:

> Finally, it is, I think, a striking feature of moral obligations that a person's being unwilling to fulfill the obligation is irrelevant to having the obligation and is also irrelevant to the adverse judgment in case the obligation is not fulfilled. Perhaps even more important is the fact that, at least for some obligations, it is also irrelevant in both these ways for one to point out that he does not see how fulfilling the obligations can do him any good. (217)

Bringing the features of a Russellian world into proximity with the concept of morality reveals the surprising aspects of morality in a Russellian world:

> I claim that in the actual world we have some obligations that, when we fulfill them, will confer on us no net Russellian benefit—in fact, they will result in a Russellian loss. If the world is Russellian, then Russellian benefits and losses are the only benefits and losses, and also then we have moral obligations whose fulfillment will result in a net loss of good to the one who fulfills them. I suggest, however, that it would be very strange to have such obligations—strange not simply in the sense of being unexpected or surprising, but in some deeper way. (217–18)

Mavrodes is very clear that he is not arguing that there is a logical contradiction between the world being a Russellian world and there being moral obligations of this type. He is arguing only that such obligations would be "queer" in such a world. They would not fit. They would be somewhat surprising. He entertains two sorts of objections to this argument. First, it is possible that he is mistaken about the nature of moral obligation. If morality is subjective in the sense that statements about obligations can be analyzed into statements about the speaker or the subject of moral judgment, then the truth of such statements could fit very well into a Russellian world. For example, if the statement "Murder is wrong" can be analyzed into the statement "I dislike murder" or "If you murder someone you will feel badly," then the moral prohibition concerning murder will be very much at home in a Russellian world.

The second objection is that it is possible that the concept of moral obligation has been described correctly, but obligations are connected not to God but to a Platonic realm of eternal forms. In this way, specific obligations might be connected to the Form of the Good. This Form exists independently of any human being's concerns or wishes. Objective moral obligations could then be grounded without a religious world being the real world. Mavrodes points out that the Platonic world is more like a theistic world than it is like the Russellian world. So Platonism might be able to ground objective moral obligations without God, but that fact will be of little comfort to those who hold our world to be a Russellian world.[20]

The argument about fittingness aims to show that moral obligations that are objectively binding upon us fit better in a theistic world than they do in a world that is atheistic. If this is the case, then the reality of moral obligations will point to God. It is striking that some leading atheist philosophers agree with Mavrodes. John Mackie has written, "If, then, there are such intrinsically prescriptive objective values, they make the existence of a god more probable than it would have been without them. Thus we have, after all, a defensible inductive argument from morality to the existence of a god."[21]

One way to unpack how moral obligations fit or fail to fit in the atheistic world is to consider the nature of obligation in general. In previously published work, the distinction was made between a hypothetical imperative (a conditional command) on the one hand and a categorical imperative (an unconditional command) on the other.[22] A hypothetical imperative expresses a certain obligation. This obligation, however, is binding only if the condition is met. Prudential decisions, etiquette, and game playing are all arenas in which obligations are hypothetical. The structure of a hypothetical imperative, which is not always transparent, is, "If you want ____, you ought to ____." We can fill in the blanks with various sorts of commands.

Parents and teachers often urge children to study hard: "If you want to do well in math, you ought to do your homework." This conditional command is a prudential one. If one is playing chess, there is another sort of hypothetical imperative: "You ought to move your bishop only on the diagonal." This rule can be seen to be conditional when it is challenged. If a player asks why he is obligated to move the bishop only on the diagonal, we would reply, "Those are the rules." So the structure of the command is, "If you want to play chess, then you ought to move your bishop only on the diagonal." If someone moves the bishop along the horizontal, then he is no longer playing chess. Rules of etiquette work in a similar way: "If you want to be polite, take smaller bites." Conditional commands are binding, as we said, only if the condition is fulfilled. A person is always free to reject the condition. If he rejects the condition, he is free not to perform the obligation. A student might say, "I don't want to do well in math." In this case, the command to study loses its traction. A player might say, "But I am not playing chess." Then he can move his bishop anywhere he likes.

A categorical imperative is an unconditional command.[23] It is one not linked to a condition. As a result one cannot escape the obligation in the same way that one can in the case of a hypothetical imperative. Moral obligation seems to be best captured by categorical rather than hypothetical imperatives. When a person is confronted with a moral obligation, there is no condition that can be rejected such that the obligation no longer holds. A moral obligation, such as "One should tell the truth," cannot be rejected by the kinds of responses that work in prudential or game-playing scenarios. Suppose a person is confronted with the obligation to tell the truth, and she replies, "But I do not care about acting morally. I am not playing the moral game." This response might explain why she chose not to tell the truth, but it will not release her from her obligation. She cannot simply opt out of the moral game. Even if she chooses not to tell the truth, the moral evaluation of her action stands. It is not removed even though she does not care to satisfy her obligation.[24]

Hypothetical imperatives are tied to specific purposes. The obligation to study is tied to the purpose of passing math, or graduating, or getting a good job. The obligation to move your bishop on the diagonal is tied to the purpose of playing chess. As we saw, these purposes can be rejected. They are, at least in some sense, up to the person who bears the obligation. One can choose not to pass or to graduate or to play chess. If conditional commands are tied to purposes, it makes sense that unconditional commands will also be tied to purposes. The moral obligation to tell the truth, then, is likely to be tied to a purpose. It is not a conditional purpose, however. Unconditional commands require unconditional purposes. Whatever the purposes are that are at work in moral obligations, they must hold for each person regardless of his particular circumstances. If there is such a purpose, it is easy to see how we could be under unconditional imperatives.

Another way to see the connection between categorical imperatives and purpose is to suppose there is no unconditional purpose for human beings. In this case it is difficult to see how there can be categorical imperatives at all. The question that is raised is, "Why should I feel like I must obey the moral rules?" As far as homework and chess are concerned, this kind of question is answered in terms of purpose. If any purpose can be rejected, then every obligation is conditional. The connection between categorical imperatives and purpose appears to be strong, but it is not one of logical entailment. It might be possible for there to be categorical imperatives of the kind discussed that are not tied to purpose, but it does not seem likely. Such imperatives would be mysterious.

The nature of morality, then, provides some good reason to think that there is a purpose to human beings and that this purpose is not invented by other people. Nor is it optional. This kind of purpose for human beings is pretty surprising if there is no God and the world is a Russellian world. Yet such a purpose is not at all surprising if God exists and created human beings. If God invented human beings, he did so for a reason or reasons. Some of these reasons may ground moral truths. For example, if God made us with moral ends in mind—if he made us so that we would embody certain virtues, for example—his setting up moral reality in the way he did makes a good deal of sense. If God has spiritual purposes for us—that we would find a relationship with him and experience him as our highest good—he may set up moral rules as guidelines for how best to do that.

While the New Atheists have engaged the questions concerning whether God is needed for people to behave morally or to know what is moral, they have not addressed the question of whether God is necessary for there to be objective, binding moral arguments. This brief discussion suggests that the nature of moral obligations is evidence for the existence of God. There is much more that can be written about this kind of argument. For example, it is always possible to reject the objectivity of moral obligations, or one could challenge the claim that the nature of moral obligation is well captured by categorical imperatives. At this point, then, this argument is not meant to be conclusive. Rather it shows that the nature of morality fits better in a theistic universe than it does in an atheistic one. We will return to the issue of the fittingness of moral obligations in a world without God in the last chapter.

In this chapter we explored the criticisms raised by the New Atheists of three of the most important arguments for God's existence. For the most part, these arguments survive these criticisms. While few people will find the ontological argument persuasive, there are versions of the cosmological argument that might be convincing to some. In addition, the existence of objective moral obligations can provide ground for reasonable belief in God. In the next chapter, we shall turn our attention to the design argument for God's existence. This argument is the one that the New Atheists take the most seriously.

CHAPTER FOUR

The Design Argument

In the last chapter, we discussed the challenges raised by the New Atheists to three traditional arguments for the existence of God. We concluded that they have not shown that these arguments are without value. There are versions of these arguments that can serve as evidence for God's existence. It was not our goal to lay out an independent case for God, even though we did defend some versions of some of the arguments. In this chapter, we shall turn our attention to how the New Atheists interact with the argument that they consider to be the most important, that is, the design argument for God's existence.

The Traditional Design Argument in Paley and Hume

William Paley is the most famous historical proponent of the design argument for God's existence. He launches his argument with a story:

> In crossing a heath, suppose I pitched my foot against a *stone*, and were asked how the stone came to be there, I might possibly answer, that, for anything I knew to the contrary, it had lain there for ever; nor would it, perhaps, be very easy to show the

absurdity of this answer. But suppose I found a *watch* upon the ground, and it should be inquired how the watch happened to be in that place, I should hardly think of the answer which I had before given,—that, for anything I knew, the watch might have always been there. Yet why should not this answer serve for the watch as well as for the stone? why is it not as admissible in the second case as in the first? For this reason, and for no other, viz., that, when we come to inspect the watch, we perceive (what we could not discover in the stone) that its several parts are framed and put together for a purpose.[1]

This story illustrates that we make inferences to design from our observations in the world on a regular basis. If a person comes upon a watch, she can see that it was built by an intelligent person with a function in mind. The same person would not conclude that the stone was similarly designed. In each of these cases, the person is being reasonable. Paley is showing that we employ a rough criterion to sort out when such inferences are reasonable and when they are not. In this story, his criterion is that when it can be observed of an item that "its several parts are framed and put together for a purpose" then we can conclude that the item is designed.

In subsequent discussion, Paley defends his claim that it is this criterion that is at work when we infer design. For example, he claims that it is not because the person already knows that watches are human artifacts that she makes the inference to design. The organization and function of the parts would ground the inference to design even if watches were unknown. In addition, even if the purpose of some of the parts of the watch could not be discerned or the watch did not keep good time, the inference to design would not be undermined. Paley's discussion of these objections anticipates some of the criticisms that the design argument faces even to this day.

Paley goes on to make meticulous observations about a variety of phenomena in nature. He aims to show that these items too are put together in such a way that the variety of parts work together for common functions. He discusses the structure of the eye, of the skeletal and circulatory systems, and of the muscles, as well as a variety of features of animal and plant life. Paley argues that each of these instances provides independent grounds for the inference to the existence of a designer. Together, these various phenomena provide a very strong cumulative case. The variety of features in the natural world that exhibit design thereby strengthens the total argument significantly:

> If there were but one watch in the world, it would not be less certain that it had a maker. If we had never in our lives seen any but one single kind of hydraulic machine, yet, if of that one kind we understood the mechanism and use, we should be as perfectly assured that it proceeded from the hand and thought and skill of a workman, as if we visited a museum of the arts, and saw collected there twenty different kinds of machines for drawing water, or a thousand different kinds of other purposes. Of this point each machine is a proof independently of all the rest. So it is with the evidences of a Divine agency. The proof is not a conclusion which lies at the end of a chain of reasoning, of which chain each instance of contrivance is only a link, and of which if one link fail, the whole falls; but it is an argument separately supplied by every separate example. An error in stating an example affects only that example. The argument is cumulative, in the fullest sense of that term. The eye proves it without the ear; the ear without the eye. The proof in each example is complete. (Paley, 1:148)

The design argument can be construed either as an argument to the best explanation or as an argument by analogy. When some system contains a series of parts that work together for a function, the best explanation for the system is that it was designed. This principle, then, is applied to various observed systems. Some of them are such that the best available explanation for their origin is design. Others do not require the appeal to design. We take the argument to be an analogy when we reason as follows: just as it is reasonable to conclude that the watch is designed, based on the interworking of its parts and its discoverable function, so it is reasonable to conclude that things like the human eye and the skeletal structure are designed based on the interworking of their parts and their functions. These two approaches overlap, but it is helpful to spell out clearly that the structure of the argument can be seen in these two ways.

Design arguments similar to Paley's have been subject to a variety of criticisms in the history of philosophy. David Hume, in his posthumously published *Dialogues Concerning Natural Religion* leveled several objections that anticipated both Paley's arguments and some of the contemporary discussion. Hume takes the design argument to be an analogy between human artifacts and the universe. The principle on which the argument works is that "similar causes prove similar effects, and similar effects similar causes."[2] So the structure of a house, having all of its parts put together for the single aim of providing shelter, is thought to be similar to the structure of the universe, or of the eye, or the skeleton. The inference is that, since there cannot be a house that is not designed by intelligent people, things in nature too must have been designed by an intelligent mind.

Hume first objects that the effects in question are significantly dissimilar, and that, therefore, the analogy is weak at best. He writes, "Every departure on either side diminishes the probability, and renders the experiment less conclusive" (Part V, 165). Hume thinks that for an analogy to be strong it must include cases that are exactly similar. The least departure from exact similarity weakens the analogy. For example, to argue by analogy from some property of the circulation of blood in a frog to the same property in a human being is strong. To argue for the same human property from the circulation of sap in a tree is weak. The dissimilarities we find as we explore the natural world, Hume thinks, undermine the strength of the analogy.

Another objection Hume raises is that the conclusion of the design argument does not require that there be a single mind that is perfect and unlimited. Since the effects are finite and imperfect, we have no right to infer that the cause is anything other than finite and imperfect itself. In addition, we cannot rule out that a variety of deities worked together to construct the universe. Our experience with houses, in fact, leads us to expect a plurality of deities. Third, Hume raises the challenge that the argument gives us no reason to stop searching for the cause of the designer. If the order and structure of the universe lead us to posit an intelligent cause, why would not the order and structure of the intelligent cause itself require explanation?

The Traditional Design Argument in Hitchens, Dennett, and Dawkins

It is not surprising that the New Atheists write more about the design argument than about any of the others. Hitchens, Dennett, and Dawkins each share an interest in highlighting how contemporary science, in the form of neo-Darwinism, undermines the rationality of belief in God. The design argument is the argument most vulnerable to objections from Darwin.

In addition to the Darwinian challenge, Hitchens raises two other objections to design arguments. He argues that things in the biological world, if they are designed, seem to be designed poorly. To appeal to a perfect designer, then, seems to be implausible. Second, he attributes our wonder at the fact that the conditions necessary for life occur on earth to vanity. These objections are developed together as follows:

> It is, indeed, only because of the frightening emptiness elsewhere that we are bound to be impressed by the apparently unique and beautiful conditions that have allowed intelligent life to occur on earth. But then, vain as we are, we would be impressed wouldn't we? This vanity allows us to overlook the implacable fact that, of the other bodies in our own solar system alone, the rest are all either far too cold to support anything recognizable as life, or far too hot. The same, as it happens, is true of our own blue and rounded planetary home, where heat contends with cold to make large tracts of it into useless wasteland, and where we have come to learn that we live, and have always lived, on a climatic knife edge. Meanwhile, the sun is getting

ready to explode and devour its dependent planets like some jealous chief or tribal deity. Some design! (80)

For Hitchens, both the vanity objection and the bad-design objection rest on the fact that only a very small percentage of the known universe is fit for the emergence of intelligent life. This fact is purported to show that it is human vanity that seeks a cosmic explanation of this extremely local fact and that the universe as a whole is not very well designed after all.

Paley himself anticipated the bad-design objection:

> Neither, secondly, would it invalidate our conclusion, that the watch sometimes went wrong, or that it seldom went exactly right. The purpose of the machinery, the design, and the designer, might be evident, and, in the case supposed, would be evident, in whatever way we accounted for the irregularity of the move-ment, or whether we could account for it or not. It is not nec-essary that a machine be perfect, in order to show with what design it was made: still less necessary, where the only question is whether it were made with any design at all. (1:51–52)

Paley's response indicates that he is content with an argument that shows the existence of a designer. He does not expect this one argument will show that the designer has all of the attributes usually ascribed to God. For example, the design inference will justify the claim that the designer is extremely powerful, but not that he is unlimited in power. Paley explains this limitation:

> We ascribe power to the Deity under the name of "omnipo-tence," the strict and correct conclusion being, that a power which could create such a world as this is, must be, beyond all comparison, greater than any which we experience in ourselves, than any which we observe in other visible agents; greater also than any which we can want, for our individual protection and preservation, in the Being upon whom we depend. It is a power, likewise, to which we are not authorized, by our observation or knowledge, to assign any limits of space or duration. (2:118)

For Paley, the designer must have enough knowledge and power to create the universe. This is quite a bit of power and knowledge, though it does not necessarily have to be without limit altogether. On the other hand, there is nothing in the design argument that requires or supports the idea that the designer has only limited knowledge or power.

The vanity objection has little bite. Whether or not it is vain to be interested in explaining the presence of conditions necessary for life does not affect whether it is a worthy investigation. The fact that it is vain to be so interested in the conditions for the possibility of human life does not show that the argument is weak. It could be argued that if these investigations reveal vanity, then every scientific or philosophical investigation does so as well.

In introducing the design argument, Dawkins claims that "[t]he argument from design is the only one still in regular use today, and it still sounds to many like the ultimate knockdown argument" (79). While there are actually many arguments in regular use, as we saw in the previous chapter, it is certain that the design argument is one of the most popular and accessible arguments. The intuition behind it is clear and common. Complicated things that work toward a function or purpose seem to be designed to do so.

Dawkins' criticisms of the argument center on Darwin's contributions. "Thanks to Darwin, it is no longer true to say that nothing we know looks designed unless it is designed" (79). The bulk of Dawkins' discussion consists of refuting various creationist claims. As far as the traditional design argument is concerned, the creationist strategy is to argue that the Darwinian account is not plausible. Dawkins spends a good deal of time refuting the various challenges to Darwinism raised both by the older style creationists and by those subscribing to intelligent design theory. If the creationist's attempt to undermine the plausibility of Darwinism is unsuccessful, then the Darwinian objection to the traditional design argument still stands.

Dennett agrees with Dawkins and calls the design argument "surely the most intuitive and popular argument" (242). As mentioned previously, he refers the reader to his discussion of the argument in *Darwin's Dangerous Idea*, chapters 1 and 7. We shall develop his criticisms of the design argument from this text. In the first of these chapters, Dennett discusses what we are calling the traditional design argument. He develops four of Hume's criticisms. The first criticism Dennett endorses is the claim that the argument embodies the fallacy of composition. Because parts of the observed universe exhibit the sort of purpose that suggests design, it does not follow that the whole universe shows the marks of design. One cannot argue from the properties of the parts to the properties of the whole. This step, Hume (and Dennett) thinks, is essential to the design argument. Second, Dennett endorses Hume's challenge that the design argument raises the question of the origin of God. If items in nature appear to be purpose-directed require design, then God surely requires design as well. If one is content not to inquire into who designed God, is it any less rational to be content not to inquire into the design of those features under discussion? Hume takes it to be an arbitrary move to demand an explanation for some items but not for God as well.

Third, Dennett observes that Hume suggests an alternative hypothesis to God, that is, that the universe was designed by a less-than-intelligent mind:

> And what surprise must we entertain, when we find him a stupid mechanic, who imitated others, and copied an art, which, through a long succession of ages, after multiplied trials, mistakes, corrections, deliberations, and controversies, had been gradually improving? Many worlds might have been botched and bungled, throughout an eternity, ere this system was struck out. (Part V, 167)

Hume's point is that the evidence for design that is available does not support the existence of God more than it does the existence of the stupid mechanic. Finally, Dennett mentions Hume's worry that the design argument does not suggest that the universe is the product of one mind. There very well could have been many designers.

Dennett endorses all of these criticisms of Hume. He thinks that they render the traditional design argument weak indeed. What is especially interesting is Dennett's discussion of Hume's conclusion. Rather than suspending judgment, Philo (the character in the dialogue thought most to represent Hume's own views) concludes:

> That the works of nature bear a great analogy to the productions of art is evident; and according to all the rules of good reasoning, we ought to infer, if we argue at all concerning them, that their causes have a proportional analogy. But as there are also considerable differences, we have reason to suppose a proportional difference in the causes; and in particular ought to attribute a much higher degree of power and energy to the supreme cause than any we have ever observed in mankind. Here then the existence of DEITY is plainly ascertained by reason. . . . No man can deny the analogies between the effects: To restrain ourselves from enquiring concerning the causes is scarcely possible: From this enquiry, the legitimate conclusion is, that the causes have also an analogy: And if we are not contented with calling the first and supreme cause a GOD or DEITY, but desire to vary the expression; what can we call him but MIND or THOUGHT, to which he is justly supposed to bear a considerable resemblance? (Part VII, 216–17; capitalization in the original)

Dennett raises the critical question of why Hume seems to capitulate. Dennett's answer is that "he *just couldn't imagine* any other explanation of the origin of the manifest design in nature" (*Darwin*, 32; emphasis in original). Dennett is probably right about Hume. All of the counterarguments to the traditional design argument could not completely undermine the strength of the analogy between natural things and artifacts. Without some plausible alternative explanation for how things could appear to be designed to accomplish various functions when they were not actually designed, it was just too difficult to think that design was not involved. Had Hume known about Darwin, he might not have kept open the possibility of a designer.

Darwinism as an Objection

While the objections that Hume raises are important to consider in defending a design argument, no objection has been as devastating for these kinds of arguments as has the rise of Darwinism. What Darwinism provided was an account of how things in nature can come to exhibit the marks of being designed without actually being designed. This account shows that the inference from the observation that the eye, for example, shows the order and function that make it look designed to the conclusion that it probably is designed is a weak inference. It is weak because we have a plausible explanation for how it can look designed without actually being designed.

It is helpful to specify exactly how Darwinism undermines the traditional design argument. Seeing its role clearly will be helpful in evaluating the modern design argument that does not make inferences based on biological observations. The Darwinian objection, as a result, can be seen as a particular objection of a certain kind. To illustrate its precise role, we ought to state clearly the content of the design inference itself. The generic design inference can be captured by this sentence:

> If some item shows that it is structured for a purpose, then it is reasonable to conclude it was designed.

The Darwinian challenge shows that this sentence is false. Despite the fact that things such as the human eye are structured for various purposes, it is not reasonable to conclude that they were designed. The reason for this assessment, as we saw, is that Darwinism has provided a plausible account of how items such as the eye can show the marks of design without actually being designed. We can see, therefore, that this version of the design inference is not valid. Showing the marks of design does not support the actuality of design.

There are still cases in everyday life where we make design inferences and we think that these inferences are valid. If they are, we ought to be able to explain the structure of a valid design inference. What we learned from the Darwinian story is that a valid design inference will need to take into account the possibility of alternative explanations of the appearance of design that do not involve actual design. A good candidate for a valid principle of inferring design is the following:

> If some item shows that it is structured for a purpose, and we have no plausible account of how it shows the marks of design without being designed, then it is reasonable to conclude it was designed.

This version of the design inference has a good chance of being true. There are two things to note. First, despite the efforts of creationists and those advocating versions of intelligent design theory in biology, Darwinism is, at the very least, a significantly plausible account that aims to show how biological phenomena show the marks of design without being designed. Therefore, it is not reasonable to infer a designer from the apparent design in things that Darwinism can explain (such as the human eye or skeletal structure). Second, even if we find an item that shows the marks of design and we have no account of how it does so without actually being designed, it does not follow that a designer must exist. It makes it reasonable to think there is a designer. A design argument, based on this sort of principle, will fall short of delivering certainty. It is always possible that an account sufficient to explain the apparent design will be found and the inference to design undermined.

Darwinism has undermined the traditional design argument. The New Atheists are certainly correct in their assessment here. The only way to salvage any sort of design argument for the existence of God is to find items that have the mark of design but are outside the scope of a Darwinian explanation. Taking this strategy is, in effect, abandoning the traditional design argument altogether. Those who take this strategy put forward what we can call the modern design argument. It is usually referred to as the *fine-tuning argument*. The fine-tuning argument is an argument that the fine tuning of the universe itself shows the marks of design.

This argument has generated a lot of discussion in recent years. Of the New Atheists, Dennett and Dawkins in particular discuss and raise criticisms of this argument.

The Modern Design Argument: Fine Tuning

The fine-tuning argument for God's existence does not rely on the appearance of design in biological systems. Rather, it looks at the fundamental structure of the universe itself and sees marks of design there. More specifically, it is based on facts recently learned in cosmology that the conditions necessary for a stable universe are extremely unlikely to have occurred by chance. Dennett provides a summary of some of these findings:

> As more and more has been learned about the development of the universe since the Big Bang, about the conditions that permitted the formation of galaxies and stars and the heavy elements from which planets can be formed, physicists and cosmologists have been more and more struck by the exquisite sensitivity of the laws of nature. The speed of light is approximately 186,000 miles per second. What if it were only 185,000 miles per second, or 187,000 miles per second? Would that change much of anything? What if the force of gravity were 1 percent more or less than it is? The fundamental constants of physics—the speed of light, the constant of gravitational attraction, the weak and strong forces of subatomic interaction, Planck's constant—have values that of course permit the actual development of the universe as we know it to have happened. But it turns out that if in imagination we change any of these values by just the tiniest amount, we thereby posit a universe in which none of this could have happened, and indeed in which apparently nothing life-like could ever have emerged: no planets, no atmospheres, no solids at all, no elements except hydrogen and helium, or maybe not even that—just some boring plasma of hot, undifferentiated stuff, or an equally boring nothingness. So, isn't it a wonderful fact that the laws are *just right* for us to exist? Indeed, one might want to add, we almost didn't make it! (*Darwin*, 164–65; emphasis in original)[3]

In discussing how Darwinism created a decisive objection to the traditional design argument, we articulated the following principle for inferring design:

> If some item shows that it is structured for a purpose, and we have no plausible account of how it shows the marks of design without being designed, then it is reasonable to conclude it was designed.

To apply this principle to the fine-tuning argument, then, is a two-step process. First we determine whether the facts appealed to in the fine-tuning argument constitute a system that appears to be structured for a purpose. If they do, then we search for a plausible account of how the physical constants could show the marks of design while not actually being designed.

The fact that there are many independent equations whose constants have to fall within a very small range in order for any universe with solid mass or any heavy elements to emerge at all, let alone biological life, is what must be explained. The fine-tuning argument for God's existence claims that it is much too improbable for our sort of universe to emerge by chance. The universe itself, then, shows the marks of design. The marks of design are not seen in its beauty or order but in the necessary conditions of its existence. In the traditional design argument, the structure of the eye, with its various parts working together for a purpose, was the item in need of explanation. That the eye had this appearance was not in dispute. How best to explain the apparent design was the matter of dispute. So too in the fine-tuning argument, the fact that the physical constants admit only a very small range of values if they are to result in any interesting universe is not subject to dispute. The dispute is, similarly, about the best explanation for this apparent design.

The objections to the claim that the apparent fine tuning of the universe points to God consist of various alternative accounts to explain what looks like fine tuning. Dennett and Dawkins discuss several of the challenges to the theistic explanation of the apparent fine tuning of the universe. Some of the challenges they raise are found throughout the literature on the subject. Rather than discussing each author independently, we shall pursue five objections in sequence.

Natural Selection as a Consciousness Raiser

Dawkins believes that natural selection is and ought to be a consciousness raiser. He writes that "[n]atural selection not only explains the whole of life; it also raises our consciousness to the power of science to explain how organized complexity can emerge from simple beginnings without any deliberate guidance" (116). Not only is natural selection a theory that explains the development of the great variety of biological species, it also attunes us to expect naturalistic explanations of phenomena outside of its own proper (biological) domain. "But Darwinian evolution, specifically natural selection . . . shatters the illusion of design within the domain of biology, and teaches us to be suspicious of any kind of design hypothesis in physics and cosmology as well" (118). Seeing natural selection as a consciousness raiser is not a specific objection to the fine-tuning argument. It is a prerequisite for any investigation into the possibility of design. We ought to enter such investigation, Dawkins thinks, already suspicious of any kind of design hypothesis.

There are two ways we can take natural selection as a consciousness raiser. The first is to hold that it provides a healthy caution for those who are quick to conclude that design is the only possible explanation for some phenomena. As we saw above, it is hard to overestimate how profound the impact of Darwinism is on the traditional design argument. What appeared to many thinkers to be obvious evidence of design in one century was widely agreed not to count at all as evidence for design in the next. The rise of Darwinism and its impact on the traditional design argument certainly is a warning to be cautious.

The second way we might take natural selection to be a consciousness raiser is to take it that no argument for design in principle can be well grounded. This sort of position might go as follows:

since natural selection has shown biological design arguments to be weak, we ought to expect that other theories will show any design argument to be weak. Therefore we ought to take them to be weak. Dawkins comes close to endorsing this stronger position when he claims that people who think that the God hypothesis is as likely as the multi-universe hypothesis (discussed below) "have not had their consciousness raised by natural selection" (146). A proper appreciation of natural selection, he thinks, ought to make us immune from the temptation to attribute anything outside of human artifacts to design.

While we can appreciate the caution that Darwinism provides, this consciousness raising does not require the rejection of the possibility of design a priori. Rather, we ought to approach design arguments on their own merit by carefully searching out alternative explanations. If none of the alternative explanations are plausible (or more plausible than design), it is reasonable to attribute the phenomena to design.

The Physical Constants Are Necessary

The second objection to the fine-tuning argument is that the argument assumes that the values of the physical constants are contingent. That is, they could have had any value within a wide range of possibilities. The argument points to the fact that these values seem to be set precisely to result in the kind of universe required for life. What if these values had to be set in the ways they were? Then there would be nothing that needed to be explained. Dawkins explains this objection:

> When we finally reach the long-hoped-for Theory of Everything, we shall see that the six key numbers depend upon each other, or on something else as yet unknown, in ways that we today cannot imagine. The six numbers may turn out to be no freer to vary than is the ratio of a circle's circumference to its diameter. It will turn out that there is only one way for a universe to be. (144)

Dawkins himself thinks that this is not a very good objection. Even if the values of the constants are set necessarily, he asks, "But why did that one way have to be such a set-up for our eventual evolution?" (144). Dawkins thinks that it is still a puzzle that the one necessary set of values of the physical constants fell within the very narrow range of values that allow intelligent life to emerge.

Most philosophers do not think that the laws of physics are necessary in the same way as the laws of logic. Concerning the idea that the theory of everything will show the values of the physical constants to be necessary, Peter van Inwagen observes,

> If the discovery of such a marvelous theory were to occur, it would all but refute the idea that the actual cosmos is one among many radically different possible cosmoi and would therefore all but refute the version of the teleological argument that we are considering. At present, however, there seems to be no particular reason to think that this is how things will turn out.[4]

Until there is specific evidence that the physical constants have their values as a matter of logical or metaphysical necessity, the notion that their values have to be set as they are does not have much to recommend it. The fact that the values of the constants appear to be contingent gives us good reason to think they are contingent, in fact.

The Anthropic Principle

The fine-tuning argument has generated a fascinating sort of response now known as the *anthropic principle*. What is fascinating is the range of interpretations and uses to which the principle is put. Dawkins observes that the question about the origin of the universe could not even be raised unless our universe was fit for life. He explains further that "[t]he anthropic answer, in its most general form, is that we could only be discussing the question in the kind of universe that was capable of producing us. Our existence therefore determines that the fundamental constants of physics had to be in their respective Goldilocks zones" (144). The

Goldilocks zone to which Dawkins refers is that zone in which the value of a constant is neither too big nor too small, but rather just right. He thinks that the anthropic principle serves as an alternative explanation for the fine tuning of the universe. There is no need, then, to appeal to a designer.

Dawkins claims that while the development of species can be explained by Darwinism, events such as the origin of the universe, the origin of life on earth, or the origin of consciousness might be explained by the anthropic principle in the following sort of way:

> There are billions of planets [Dawkins is presuming here, for the sake of a larger argument] that have developed life at the level of bacteria, but only a fraction of these life forms ever made it across the gap to something like the eucaryotic cell. And of these, a yet smaller fraction managed to cross the later Rubicon to consciousness. If both of these are one-off events, we are not dealing with a ubiquitous and all-pervading *process*, as we are with ordinary, run-of-the-mill biological adaptation. The anthropic principle states that, since we are alive, eucaryotic and conscious, our planet has to be one of the intensely rare planets that has bridged all these gaps. (140–41; emphasis in original)

How the principle, as articulated by Dawkins, serves as an explanation for the origin of life or of consciousness is mysterious. What it clearly does explain is that we can find ourselves only in a universe that has eucaryotic cells and consciousness.

Dennett summarizes the principle: "According to the Anthropic Principle, we are entitled to infer facts about the universe and its laws from the undisputed fact that we (we *anthropoi*, we human beings) are here to do the inferring and observing" (*Darwin*, 165). He points out that the principle has its weak version and its strong version. The weak form can be seen in an example. "If consciousness depends on complex physical structures, and complex structures depend on large molecules composed of elements heavier than hydrogen and helium, then, since we are conscious, the world must contain such elements" (165). He is careful to point out the scope of the *must* in this sentence. The proper placement of the *must* is as follows: "*It must be the case that*: if consciousness depends . . . then, since we are conscious, the world *contains* such elements" (*Darwin*, 165; emphasis and ellipse in original). It cannot be concluded that the world was necessitated to contain heavy elements, but it can be concluded with certainty that it does contain them.

The strong version of the principle takes it that the fact of consciousness makes it necessary that the world contain heavy elements. Rather than the structure of the claim being "*It must be the case that*: if consciousness depends . . . then, since we are conscious the world *contains* such elements," the strong form would claim, "If consciousness depends . . . then, since we are conscious *it must be the case that* the world contains such elements." John Barrow and Frank Tipler articulate a definition of the strong anthropic principle in precisely this way:

> Strong Anthropic Principle (SAP): The Universe must have those properties which allow life to develop within it at some stage in its history.[5]

Dennett rightly rejects this form as a "simple mistake in logic" (*Darwin*, 165). Dennett's analysis of the logical mistake highlights what is wrong with Dawkins' use of the principle. Dennett's understanding of the weak version can be captured in a broader principle of metaphysics that "if it is actual, it is possible." Whatever is the case is such that it is a real possibility. If it is a fact that we are conscious, then we know that the universe in which we exist is capable of having conscious beings. The strong version, according to Dennett, would be captured by the metaphysical principle that "if it is actual, it is necessary." If someone interprets the strong version of the anthropic principle in this way, the necessity at work cannot merely be physical necessity. It must be something like metaphysical necessity. After all, what is deemed to be necessary is the emergence of a universe with the laws of physics similar to ours. It cannot be that the emergence of these laws is necessary based on these same laws. The necessity is stronger than physical necessity. The general principle, "If it is actual, it is necessary," however, is clearly false. It does appear that Dawkins interprets the anthropic principle in the strong way that Dennett cautions against taking.

It is helpful to try to keep clear what it is precisely that wants explanation. If we want to explain, on the one hand, why the universe can sustain conscious life, appeal to the anthropic principle has nothing to offer. It amounts to the following claim: "The universe does sustain conscious life, therefore, we can know that it emerged to be able to do so. This is the explanation." It seems as though Dawkins is taking this route. The explanation for certain features of our universe, Dawkins implies, is the fact that we exist in it. If we want to explain, on the other hand, why it is that the universe in which we find ourselves is the kind of universe that can sustain conscious life, the anthropic principle reminds us that this kind of universe is the only kind in which we could find ourselves.

Perhaps a parallel case can make the problem clear. Suppose someone proposes a Darwinian account as an explanation for how human beings emerged on earth. One could imagine that the anthropic objection could go as follows: "An alternative explanation for the emergence of human beings on earth can be found by employing the anthropic principle. 'Since we are alive, eucaryotic, and conscious, our planet has to be one of the intensely rare planets that has bridged all these gaps.' Therefore, I do not need to adopt the Darwinian explanation." This employment of the anthropic principle does not offer an alternative explanation. It is simply a restatement of the fact that requires explanation. The Darwinian account explains how it is that beings that are alive, eucaryotic, and conscious could have emerged.

Mathematician Brandon Carter, who first coined the term *anthropic principle*, claims that the anthropic principle *can* play a role in providing an explanation for the fine tuning of the universe:

It is of course always philosophically possible—as a last resort, when no stronger physical argument is available—to promote a *prediction* based on the strong anthropic principle to the status of an *explanation* by thinking in terms of a "world ensemble." By this I mean an ensemble of universes characterized by all conceivable combinations of initial conditions and fundamental constants . . . The existence of any organism describable as an observer will only be possible for certain restricted combinations of the parameters, which distinguish within the world-ensemble an exceptional *cognizable* subset.[6]

This point introduces the next two challenges to the design argument. Each of them is a version of the multi-universe theory, built on the claim that there is a vast plurality of actual universes. The anthropic principle implies that we can observe only those universes that are suitable for the existence of observers, and it shows that there is a built-in observation-selection effect at work in all of our investigations of the universe. Only universes that are fit for the development of conscious life can be observed. Even if there is a multitude of universes, it is not surprising that we would observe one that is fine tuned. Furthermore, the fact that we cannot observe other universes does not provide specific evidence that ours is the only universe. If the multi-universe theory is true, we would expect the same limitations to our observations as we find in actuality. While it seems paradoxical to talk about a plurality of universes, we can differentiate between what John Leslie calls the *small-u universes* and the *capital-U Universe* (1). A small-u universe is one system in which all events and objects are interrelated in space and time and can be traced back to a single big bang. The capital-U Universe is the totality of reality. If there are two or more small-u universes, then they are all contained in the capital-U Universe. If there is only one small-u universe, then it is identical with the capital-U Universe.

The anthropic principle, although it has been employed as a kind of response to the design inference concerning the apparent fine tuning of the universe, finds its relevance as an alternative explanation only in conjunction with the multi-universe hypothesis. It does not provide any independent ground for thinking that there is no designer or that the apparent fine tuning does not point to the existence of God.

Multiple Universe I: An Evolving Series of Universes

There are different ways of positing a multitude of universes that can provide an alternate account for the apparent fine tuning of the physical constants. The first is one that resembles closely a Darwinian theory of universe development by natural selection. Both Dawkins and Dennett refer to the work of Lee Smolin,[7] who has proposed a succession of universes, each of which gives rise to offspring. Dennett elaborates:

> The basic idea is that the singularities known as black holes are in effect the birthplaces of offspring universes, in which the fundamental physical constants would differ slightly, in random ways, from the physical constants in the parent universe. . . . Those universes that just happened to have physical constants that encouraged the development of black holes would *ipso facto* have more offspring, which would have more offspring and so forth. (*Darwin*, 177)

Neither Dawkins nor Dennett put much weight on Smolin's proposal. Dawkins admits, "Not all physicists are enthusiastic about Smolin's idea, although the Nobel Prize–winning physicist Murray Gell-Mann is quoted as saying: 'Smolin: Is he that young guy with those crazy ideas? He may not be wrong'" (146). Dennett's verdict is that "it is hard to know what to make of this idea yet . . ." (*Darwin*, 178). Dennett does point out that Smolin's theory can serve as a caution to those who would claim that nothing but God could explain the fine tuning of the universe.

If such a theory could become established, it would do a lot to undermine the design inference based on the apparent fine tuning of the universe. From Dennett's description, it is unclear how the offspring universes are related to the parent universes. There needs to be a mechanism by which the offspring universes continue to share the features of their parent universes. If the physical constants in each universe differ randomly, how is it that they also differ only slightly? There must be constraints from universe to universe that limit the variation in the constants between universes. These constraints would function in a way that is similar to the way the transmission of genes functions. The range of genetic combinations found in offspring is limited by the original genes of the parents, allowing, of course, for the occasional mutation. Any mechanism that links these universes in this way will be causal. Causal links between universes seem to require shared properties of objects or laws of physics. It could be argued as well that the kind of causal interaction required by this notion implies that the universes share the same space and time. If there are shared properties and shared space and time, and there is causal interaction of any kind between them, it is difficult to justify calling the offspring different universes. They would seem to be part of the same universe. To be sure, these challenges might be able to be resolved with more work. Smolin's ideas amount to an interesting conjecture that would, if verified, be relevant to the strength of the design argument. At this point, this probably ought not be considered a plausible alternative to the design hypothesis.

Multiple Universe II: Probability Factors

The more common use of multiple universes in response to the fine-tuning arguments is to argue that the odds against our universe arising by chance need not be so small as to render it unlikely. Consider again the facts appealed to in this argument. There are many equations describing independent factors that are necessary for the formation of heavy elements, planets, and other conditions necessary for life. The values of the constants in these equations must fall within a very narrow range if such a universe is to emerge. The probability of all of these constants having values within the correct range appears to be astronomically small. Therefore, it is reasonable, so the argument goes, to think that these values were set by design. The multi-universe response aims at undermining the reasonability of the design inference. Dennett illustrates this version of the multi-universe response with a story:

> Suppose you were to create a ten round coin-tossing tournament without letting each of the 1,024 "contestants" realize he was entered in a tournament. You say to each one as you recruit him: "Congratulations, my friend. I am Mephistopheles, and I am going to bestow great powers on you. With me at your side, you are going to win ten consecutive coin-tosses without a loss!" You then arrange for your dupes to meet, pairwise, until you have a final winner. (You never let the contestants discuss your relation to them, and you kiss off the 1,023 losers along the way with some *sotto voce* gibe to the effect that they were pretty gullible to believe your claim about being Mephistopheles!) The winner—and there must be one—will certainly have been given evidence of being a Chosen One, but if he falls for it, this is simply an illusion of what we might call retrospective myopia. The winner doesn't see that the situation was structured so that somebody simply had to be the lucky one—and he just happened to be *it*. (*Darwin*, 179–80; emphasis in original)

This story illustrates the effect of a multi-universe theory on the design inference. Suppose our universe was one of several trillion universes (we can make the number as large as needed) that were "launched" randomly, with the values of the physical constants set randomly. The fact that our universe has the conditions that are necessary for life would seem highly improbable to us. It would turn out, however, to be likely that some universe or other would be able to sustain life. We just happen to be the lucky ones!

In this scenario, the overwhelming majority of universes would collapse nearly instantly or expand so rapidly that there would be no star formation. In other words, the vast majority of universes would have no chance of biological life. If trillions of universes were generated, however, it would not be surprising that eventually a very few would be fit for stars and planets and the other conditions for biological life. The probability that any particular universe could be life sustaining is extremely small. The probability that some universe or other could be so would be pretty high (as long as enough universes are generated).

The upshot of the notion of multiple universes is that, if there really are enough universes that vary randomly, it is not unlikely that one or two would be able to sustain life. The appeal to design thought to be required to explain the values of the physical constants turns out not to be necessary. The multitude of universes does provide an account of how the fine tuning can appear to be a result of design when it is not actually designed. As such, the multi-universe story might undermine the design inference. It remains to be seen how plausible this alternative account turns out to be.

We can summarize the role of the multi-universe objection to the fine-tuning argument by rehearsing two steps in the discussion. First, the theist points out that fine tuning cannot come about by chance since the probabilities are too small. The atheist, in response, claims that the theist's claim would be true *if* ours is the only universe. If there are a vast number of universes, then the apparent fine tuning of our universe can be explained by chance. As William Lane Craig points out, "The Many-Worlds Hypothesis is a sort of backhanded compliment to the design hypothesis in its recognition that fine tuning cries out for explanation."[8] It is important to realize that the atheist rebuttal to the argument is not without significant cost. The atheist has to believe that there exist, in reality, trillions of universes. If there is only one universe, or if there are a very few universes, then the design inference is strong. It also ought to be noted that the multi-universe hypothesis is not compatible with the claim that the constants are necessary.

What is the evidence that there exists a vast multitude of universes? Dennett mentions the suggestion of John Archibald Wheeler that "the universe oscillates back and forth for eternity: a Big Bang is followed by expansion, which is followed by contraction into a Big Crunch, which is followed by another Big Bang, and so forth forever, with random variations in the constants and other crucial parameters occurring in each oscillation" (*Darwin*, 179).

As far as evidence for this conjecture is concerned, Dennett seems skeptical: "It is *hard to believe* that this idea is empirically testable in any meaningful way, but we should reserve judgment. Variations or elaborations on the theme *just might have* implications that *could be* confirmed or disconfirmed" (179; emphasis added).

Many objections have been raised to the multi-universe theories. Robin Collins argues that while most such theories are entirely speculative, Steven Weinberg's inflationary model "does have a reasonable basis in current physics."[9] This model is based on the notion that the rate of expansion of the universe, shortly after the big bang, briefly exceeded the speed of light. This supposition is an attempt to solve a series of problems in standard big bang theory. To explain the formation of many universes with varied physical constants, however, Collins argues that there must be some physical mechanism to cause this variation. While this requirement is not enough to reject the multi-universe hypothesis, he claims that "[a] better response is to note that the 'many-universe generator' itself, whether that given by chaotic inflationary models or some other type, seems to need to be 'well-designed' in order to produce life-sustaining universes" (143). Even if there is some kind of random universe generator, it will resemble a human artifact and thus will require an explanation for how it functions and why it functions in a way to make universes that are fit for life. Collins goes on to point out that the functioning of an inflationary universe generator requires precise background laws to be in place:

> For example, without the Pauli-exclusion principle, electrons would occupy the lowest atomic orbit and hence complex and varied atoms would be impossible; or, without a universally attractive force between all masses, such as gravity, matter would not be able to form sufficiently large material bodies (such as planets) for life to develop or for long-lived stable energy sources such as stars to exist. The universe generator hypothesis, however, does not explain these background laws. (144)

William Lane Craig argues that "the Many-Worlds Hypothesis is no more scientific, and no less metaphysical, than the hypothesis of a Cosmic Designer" (171). This claim might seem controversial. Martin Rees, in the same volume, defends the scientific nature of these hypotheses:

> Science is an experimental or observational enterprise, and it is natural to be troubled by assertions that invoke something inherently unobservable. Some might regard the other universes as being in the province of metaphysics rather than physics. But I think they already lie within the proper purview of science. It is not absurd or meaningless to ask "Do unobservable universes exist?" even though no quick answer is likely to be forthcoming. The question plainly can't be settled by direct observation, but evidence can be sought that could lead to an answer.[10]

Rees points to two items in his admittedly brief defense of the scientific nature of the multi-universe hypothesis. First, he observes that the question of the existence of unobservable universes is not a meaningless question. Second, he claims that it is a question for which one could seek evidence. His position here is reminiscent of Dawkins' claim that the God hypothesis is a scientific claim. If all it takes for a question to be a scientific question is for it not to be meaningless and to be one for which evidence can be sought, then every metaphysical question is also scientific. It may turn out that the multi-universe hypothesis will be supported by the kind of evidence that counts unambiguously as scientific. In the meantime, however scientific we want to think it is, it is in large part a metaphysical theory as well. Given that it posits unverifiable domains, it is likely to remain largely metaphysical, whatever strictly scientific evidence might become available.

Not much should rest on labeling a claim scientific or metaphysical. Both, as we have seen, are arenas where evidence is relevant to the reasonability of holding one theory over the alternatives. The quest to label this hypothesis scientific, it seems, has more to do with the rhetorical strength of pitting a "scientific" theory against a religious or metaphysical one. It is also important to consider that the boundaries of what counts as a scientific theory change over time. Early modern science, in the time of

Descartes and Galileo, had no room for forces such as electro-
magnetism. Science had to expand her boundaries in the wake
of evidence. Newtonian mechanics had no room for the relativity
posited by Einstein. It might turn out that the boundaries of science will expand to make room for unobservable universes for
which no direct empirical evidence is possible. At this point, however, we do well to recognize that the multi-universe theory is as
metaphysical as it is scientific.

Roger White has leveled another objection to the multi-
universe hypothesis.[11] He admits that the hypothesis does make
it less mysterious that some universe would be life permitting. It
does nothing, however, to make it less mysterious that this very
universe (the one that happened to be fit to allow us to be here)
can sustain life. Although White puts his argument forth by using
probability calculus, he illustrates it with a story:

> Suppose I'm wondering why I feel sick today, and someone sug-
> gests that perhaps Adam got drunk last night. I object that I have
> no reason to believe this hypothesis since Adam's drunkenness
> would not raise the probability of *me* feeling sick. But, the reply
> goes, it does raise the probability that *someone* in the room feels
> sick, and we know that this is true, since we know that you feel
> sick, so the fact that someone in the room feels sick is evidence
> that Adam got drunk. Clearly something is wrong with this rea-
> soning. Perhaps if all I knew (by word of mouth, say) was that
> someone or other was sick, this would provide some evidence
> that Adam got drunk. But not when I know specifically that *I*
> feel sick. . . . What has gone wrong here seems to be a failure
> to consider the *total evidence* available to us. (233; emphasis in
> original)

The fact that our universe is fine tuned does imply that some
universe is fine tuned. The multi-universe hypothesis can support
that some universe or other is fit for life. It does not, White thinks,
do anything to lessen the improbability of the very thing for which
we want an explanation. Why is our universe (as opposed to some
universe or other) such that life is possible?

Dennett thinks that the multi-universe theory is sufficient to undermine the strength of the fine-tuning design argument:

> In the meantime, it is worth noting that this family of hypotheses does have the virtue of extending the principles of explanation that work so well in testable domains all the way out. Consistency and simplicity are in its favor. And that, once again, is certainly enough to blunt the appeal of the traditional alternative. (*Darwin*, 179)

Dennett's claim that this theory blunts the design inference is premature. It is not the bare existence of an alternative explanation for the apparent fine tuning that will undermine the argument for design. That account must be plausible if it is "to blunt the appeal of the traditional alternative." We have investigated several objections to the plausibility of the multi-universe theory. Even if the theory becomes plausible, as Roger White has argued, the existence of trillions of universes does not lessen the improbability that our universe is the one fine tuned for life.

Although the multi-universe theory is not sufficient to undermine the argument for design, it does make it less strong than it otherwise would have been. If independent evidence is found that makes the theory more likely than the design hypothesis, then the fine-tuning argument will be undermined. As it stands at this point, however, the apparent fine tuning in the universe makes it more likely that our universe was designed than that it was the product of chance. This argument has not fallen to the criticisms of the New Atheists.

≡

CHAPTER FIVE

Darwinian Stories of Religion

[handwritten annotations: "broadly Darwinian" Explination]

Both Dawkins and Dennett argue that it is possible to explain the rise and nature of religious belief and practice through a kind of broadly Darwinian account. Their account can be called "broadly Darwinian" because their account is not one that is limited to biological matters. It includes elements of anthropology, meme theory, and sociology. This sort of intellectual endeavor has a lot to commend it. Careful attention, however, ought to be paid to the use for which this sort of exercise can be put. What conclusions can reasonably be drawn from their theorizing? After we discuss Dennett's and Dawkins' accounts of the Darwinian story of religion, we will explore how this investigation can play a role in various kinds of arguments about the truth or reasonableness of religious belief.

The General Outline of the Darwinian Story

There are two fundamental features of a Darwinian theory of anything. The first is the payoff. In a Darwinian account, the feature that is to be explained must result in, or be connected with something else that results in, some survival benefit. The reason that opposable thumbs can be accounted for in a Darwinian story is that it is plausible that there is a payoff for opposable thumbs. Having such thumbs increases the ability of an animal to grasp things such as food and sticks. The ability to walk erect has the payoff of being able to see greater distances, so the animal can find food and avoid predators more effectively.

The second feature of any Darwinian story is that the features to be explained must be transmitted from one generation to the next. In the biological theory, features are transmitted by genes. The discovery of genes propelled Darwin's original theory to a new level of confirmation. It provided us with a powerful mechanism to explain the transmission of traits as well as the occasional appearance of deviations from the ordinary hereditary results. Most items are passed from generation to generation unchanged. Once in awhile, a new feature results from a mutation and is passed to the next generation. Variations almost always hinder the survival of the organism with the variation. Occasionally, however, these new features are beneficial to the organism. In such cases, the new feature might eventually become part of a new "normal" genotype (and phenotype) of the species.

Darwinian stories of the rise and nature of religious belief and practice, then, must include both the payoff and the mechanism of transmission. Explaining each of these features constitutes the bulk of the work in articulating particular versions of these theories. In order to evaluate a Darwinian story, we must assess how strong the explanations of the payoff and transmission turn out to be.

The general Darwinian story of the origin of religious beliefs and practices can be told very simply. Religious belief emerged as people habitually ascribed minds and mental activity to both animate and inanimate objects such as trees, stars, and weather phenomena. This attribution became the foundation for certain shared practices that gave local human communities a degree of internal cooperation and shared identity that they would not have had otherwise. The strong shared identity and the higher degree of cooperation allowed the community to work together more effectively for survival. Those communities with unifying beliefs and practices survived, and the communities without such beliefs and practices did not.

One strength of Dawkins' and Dennett's employment of this analysis is that they do not rely merely on the simple summary of such an account. They dig more deeply into the literature and into the nuances of what any such account would have to include in order for it to be plausible.

Dennett's Version

Dennett makes the most use of the Darwinian story of religion. In fact, *Breaking the Spell* can be summarized as an extended argument for researching religion by appeal to Darwinian means and resources. Dennett aims to summarize what he calls the *"best current version* of the story science can tell about how religions have become what they are" (103). He is careful to add, "I am not claiming that this is what science has already established about religion. The main point of this book is to insist that we don't yet know—but we can discover—the answers to these important questions if we make a concerted effort" (103). This admission helps us better understand his approach. It would be unfair to ascribe to Dennett a belief in the particulars of any of the Darwinian accounts he describes. His project is not to explain how it is that religious belief and practice actually emerged. Rather, he aims to explain why it is plausible to think that this emergence can be (and eventually will be) explained in a Darwinian manner. If the accounts he presents are plausible, then we ought to think that there may be a good explanation that will eventually be fairly well confirmed. The best current version of the story science can tell, however, is still largely a speculative story. The speculative nature of these explanations must be kept in mind in order not to presume there is more evidence for them than there actually is.

Two parts of Dennett's story play particularly strong roles. These are the intentional stance and a predilection for memorable stories.

The Intentional Stance

Human beings have a disposition to see agents or other minds in the world. In fact, we have the tendency to ascribe mentality to things even when we know they are not conscious agents. In Dennett's words, we take up the "intentional stance."[1] The intentional stance is a posture we take when we treat other things in the world as agents that have beliefs about the world and that have specific desires. In treating these things as agents, we expect that they will act in accordance with their beliefs and desires.

We may take up the intentional stance when we explain, for example, why earthworms come to the surface after the rain. We may say, "They want to get out where they can breathe." While it is true that worms need to breathe and that rain-soaked earth makes breathing difficult, to say that they want to get out implies that they have desires and beliefs. They desire to breathe, and they believe that coming to the surface will make breathing possible. To say that the thermostat shuts off the heat because it wants to maintain the right temperature in the room is to apply the intentional stance to a relatively simple, inanimate artifact.

Now, we know that earthworms and thermostats do not have conscious mental states the way we do. Ascribing such mental states is not done literally. If we are asked whether we think that the worms really have desires, most of us will recognize that we use this language as a shortcut or as a metaphor for the nonconscious processes that allow the earthworm to modify its behavior to fit changing environmental conditions. Despite the recognition that the use of the intentional stance is metaphorical or shorthand, it is remarkable how deeply this practice is embedded in our mental habits.

The fact that human beings have a deeply embedded disposition to take the intentional stance may be relevant in the rise of religious belief in the following ways. First of all, we tend to see agents everywhere. This tendency does bring a direct survival benefit. It is important to identify those things in the environment that are dangerous to our survival. By treating such things as agents, we internalize general patterns of behavior that help us anticipate danger. Second, we are not always aware that we take up the intentional stance as a shortcut. In many cases, we may not know whether the thing is an agent or not. The habit of ascribing agency to inanimate and nonconscious things such as storms, harvests, trees, and even dead ancestors can give rise to beliefs in their actual agency. These beliefs can easily lead to the desire to influence or persuade agents to behave in ways we want them to behave. We can try to placate a violent storm or appease a dead ancestor. It is not difficult to see how some primitive religious beliefs could have their roots in these habits.

What we are calling a *belief* here might not be a conscious belief at all. It does not begin as a clearly articulated doctrine. In fact, at this point in the development of his account, Dennett thinks that it is not yet an actual belief. He prefers to call it a hunch or a "captivating morsel of a story line" (124). The origin of religion might have its roots in the habitual taking of natural phenomena to be agents that have a supernatural character or origin. When people reflect on these habits of "taking things to be agents," their hunches solidify into conscious beliefs in a more robust sense.

Memorable Stories

Dennett thinks that the habit of taking the intentional stance might also give rise to a predilection for certain kinds of stories. Once we begin to see the trees, storms, and mountains, for example, as agents, we have the raw materials of a robust mythology. Trees walk, mountains are giants, storms are our enemies! (Think of the stone giants in chapter 4 of J. R. R. Tolkien's *The Hobbit*.)

Although these thoughts (that the storm awakens the giants of the mountain and they are hurling boulders at us) will almost always be fleeting, occasionally some of these thoughts stick and become stories. Stories can be developed and retold and become part of the identity and culture of a family or tribe. One of the payoffs of a strong tendency toward stories is that it contributes to increased memory. Having a story about storms helps us remember what they are and how they act. It also helps us develop habits of attempting to respond to or to manipulate the action in the story.

Both Dennett and Dawkins appropriate the notion of memes in articulating how stories can be transmitted and have payoff. A meme, in brief, is the cultural analogue of a gene. It is a basic unit of cultural matter that can be preserved and passed on and that can be subject to "mutation." The concept of the meme was introduced by Dawkins in his book *The Selfish Gene*.[2] There is no strong consensus on whether the study of memes ought to be considered a hard science like genetics or if it is better thought of as a social science, more like sociology, or even as an extended metaphor. Despite this lack of consensus, many current thinkers find the concept of the meme helpful. For our purposes, it will not be necessary to determine whether meme theory is a science or whether it brings real explanatory advantage. We will be able to employ memes and talk about memes, at the very least, as a metaphor for how cultural elements are transmitted and modified over time.

Think of a certain cultural habit such as shaking hands. It has been argued that the practice of shaking hands began as a way to greet a stranger and to let him know that you carried no weapon. You extended your empty right hand to the stranger, and he did the same. This practice has spread (from whatever its actual origins) throughout many cultures. Modifications such as "giving five" and the "high five" are much more recent variations. Shaking hands, in all of its variations, is a good example of a meme.

One contribution of talking about memes is that it helps us remember that many cultural beliefs and practices are passed on and modified unconsciously. In the Buena Vista film *The Chronicles of Narnia: The Lion, the Witch, and the Wardrobe*[3] there is a scene in which the girl, Lucy, meets the faun, Tumnus, in Narnia. Lucy holds out her hand to shake hands. Tumnus hesitates, not knowing what to do. She says, "You shake it." Tumnus asks, "Why?" Lucy responds, a little bewildered, "I don't know." Memes can be practiced and passed on unconsciously.

Religious belief and practice, or at least the rudiments of unconscious belief and habitual practice, could have taken root in a community as memes became embedded in memorable stories. As parents retell the stories to their children, the stories take on more coherence and form. Eventually, some stories are considered true, and a fuller notion of belief or moral identity has developed. Again, Dennett is cautious not to claim more than a level of plausibility for this idea of the emergence of religion: "Do we know that something like this fantasy-generating process has been taking place in our species for thousands of years? No, but it is a serious possibility to investigate further" (121).

Another contribution of meme theory is that it allows selection to work on the content of belief as it occurs in an individual or family or tribe. Once people become reflective about what they hold to be important or true, they regard the content of these items as worth preserving, teaching, and, in some cases, fighting for. It is not simply the brain chemistry that determines how beliefs are held and transmitted. The content of the beliefs and doctrines can play a role as well. Only if people think a cause is worthy will they sacrifice for it. People think some cause is worthy because of the content of that cause. The content of the cause must have some causal efficacy. Meme theory has the potential to explain the causal efficacy of elements in human culture, such as beliefs or stories, without being eliminativist or reductionist about their content. When it comes to religion, meme theory helps the investigator hold that the ideas themselves can have causal efficacy without also holding that they must have a supernatural origin.

Dawkins' Version

Dawkins also suggests a Darwinian account of the rise and nature of religious belief and practice. His approach shares many of the features of Dennett's discussion. He too emphasizes the relevance of our predilection to take the intentional stance and the possibility of a meme-theoretical mechanism for the distribution and inheritance of cultural practices and beliefs. Dawkins calls the payoff the "Darwinian benefit." A Darwinian benefit of some inheritable trait is the enhanced survival of the organism's genes. A Darwinian benefit might not be a direct benefit to the organism itself, as long as it helps in the survival of the organism's genes. Dawkins examines the possible sources for the Darwinian benefit of religious belief and practice. First, he considers whether religion provides direct survival advantages. He concludes that it does not, at least in any clear way. As a result, he considers two models that might explain the indirect advantages of religion. These are *group selection* and *religion as a by-product*.

Group Selection

Group selection is the notion that natural selection can work on groups as well as on individuals. We can summarize how group selection is said to work with a story given by Dawkins. A tribe with a warrior god who instructs the tribe members that they will be rewarded for bravery will be more successful in battle against tribes that have either peace-loving gods or no gods at all. Thus whatever elements (memes or other items functionally analogous to genes) gave rise to belief in the warrior gods will survive and spread, while those that gave rise to peaceful gods will tend to die out. In this story the tribe itself, rather than an individual, is the basic unit of selection. Group selection could explain how beliefs and practices that happen to emerge can take hold in a tribe or a community. It explains further how these traits can spread from tribe to tribe. As a result, it might provide the kind of resources for a good Darwinian account of religion.

Dawkins is skeptical that group selection is a real factor in Darwinian selection, however. Although he is cautious not to put too much emphasis on his own views, he lists some objections to attributing much efficacy to the notion. First, he claims that it is easy to identify certain scenarios as group selection that are in fact cases of kin altruism or reciprocal altruism.

For example, an animal (such as a mother bird) might sacrifice its life for its offspring. In a case like this one, the genes of the offspring survive. Those genes share much in common with the mother's genes. There is no question that the development of the disposition to sacrifice for one's offspring bestows a Darwinian benefit. This scenario might look like a case of group selection, but according to Dawkins it is not. It is an example of kin altruism. It is not that the flock of birds with the trait of altruism is selected as a group over flocks that do not have this trait. The individual bird that has the altruistic trait is selected for. A Darwinian explanation for the kin altruistic behavior shows that it is an advantage (specifically to the survival of her genes) that she sacrifices her life for her offspring.

Another challenge Dawkins raises to appealing to group selection as an explanation for the self-sacrificing behavior is, as he says, that such explanations are "always vulnerable to subversion from within" (171). To illustrate his point, Dawkins modifies the story of the warring tribe by including a single selfish warrior. This warrior will hold back in the battle in order to protect himself. Since the majority of the army fights with the approved zeal, his holding back will have little effect on the total outcome of the battle. In this case, his tribe gains very nearly all the benefits of the warrior god, but he will suffer far fewer risks. An individual with the disposition of our reluctant warrior has a greater chance of survival than any individual without the reluctance. We expect that such reluctance will spread throughout the population and undermine the tribal disposition to bravery.

In this way, the selection activity operating on the individual level has more effect on the population than the selection activity on the group as a whole. Whatever factors in group selection that favor self-sacrifice will be undermined in individual selection. Since the mechanisms for selection (reproduction and death) occur more rapidly and more frequently on an individual level than they do on a tribal level, it is questionable whether group selection would play a more significant role in evolution than individual selection.

Religion as a By-product of Something Else

Dawkins suggests another way to look at Darwinian stories. He suggests that to ask about the survival value of something we want to explain might be to ask the wrong question. Perhaps the item in question is connected to some other feature that has survival value. Rather than taking the rise and development of religious belief and practice as being due to group selection, Dawkins prefers the view that it is not religion itself that provides the Darwinian benefit. Rather, religion is a by-product of other things that provide the benefit.

One interesting example of this sort of behavioral by-product is introduced by Dawkins. He explains why moths habitually fly into streetlights or candle flames. Having local lights at night is a relatively recent occurrence. For millions of years, the only night lights were the moon and stars. These objects are far enough away that the light rays that reach earth are nearly parallel. Since insects use celestial objects to steer in a straight line, it is no wonder a local light such as a candle would throw them into confusion. The behavior of moths of flying into the flame is a by-product of something with survival value—the ability to navigate by stars. We could say that it is a misfiring of behavior patterns that originated in the context of a direct Darwinian benefit.

To what could religious belief and practice be related as a by-product? Dawkins here, like Dennett in his turn, is appropriately cautious. He is not claiming to have discovered the feature that truly is connected to religion in this way. He is suggesting the kind of thing that might make this approach plausible.

His suggestion about the kind of thing to which religion might be a by-product concerns how children are raised to gain the learning and experience of past generations. He explains that children could be left to discover for themselves what is safe and what is not. It is a selection advantage, however, if they can learn the rules for safe living from others. It is better from a Darwinian vantage point if they can be told not to swim in crocodile-infested waters and if they believe what they are told.

Perhaps human beings evolved so that children have a built in tendency to believe without question whatever adults in authority tell them. This tendency will help them survive. They will believe it is better to avoid crocodiles, rattlesnakes, cliffs, and poisons.

How religion might be connected with this tendency is not hard to imagine. If an adult says, "Sacrifice a goat so the rains will not fail," the children will believe there is a connection between the sacrifice and the rain. These kinds of beliefs can be propagated with as much efficiency as the rule, "Do not swim with the crocodiles." This theory does not explain the rise of the notion that the goat ought to be sacrificed, but it can explain how such notions can take hold and spread within a tribe and across tribes. This kind of explanation of how religious belief and practice develop has an advantage, Dawkins thinks, in that it gives rise to the expectation that geographically isolated groups will have different sets of arbitrary beliefs and behavior. This distribution, he claims, is exactly what we find.

Dawkins suggests other kinds of facts to which religion might possibly be related as a by-product. There are at least two ways, he suggests, that religion could be connected with the disposition to take up the intentional stance. First, the disposition to take up the intentional stance can lead to a predisposition to mind-body dualism. This position holds that the mind is not a physical thing but a mental substance that interacts somehow with the body. Predispositions to dualism make a person ripe for some kind of theism. Once the idea of a nonphysical mind is accepted, it is not an odd or striking thing that there could be some kind of nonhuman mind that is also nonphysical. A second predisposition connected to the intentional stance is the habit of taking everything (or most things) to have intrinsic purposes. The widespread attribution of teleology, Dawkins thinks, also makes human beings primed candidates for religious belief.

These features related to the intentional stance are misfirings in the way that the disposition of moths to fly into the streetlight is a misfiring. The moth flies into the streetlight because it has a certain mechanism that is functioning properly but was not developed for an environment filled with local night lights. The Darwinian benefit that gave rise to the mechanism has to do with navigation. In the environment of local night lights, that mechanism misfires. The dualist and the teleologist attribute nonphysical minds and purpose to things that do not have minds or purpose. This habit is a misfiring of a mechanism that arose for the Darwinian benefit of helping people avoid dangerous situations. Theism, on this view, might have emerged and spread because of some significant misfiring of an otherwise helpful set of dispositions.

Again, the claim that religion arose as a by-product to these other mechanisms is put forward merely as a suggestion about the kind of things that might enter into a complete or well-established Darwinian theory of religious belief and practice. Dawkins is not claiming that these suggestions are already well established.

What We Learn from Darwinian Stories of Religion

An evaluation of Dennett and Dawkins in their employment of the Darwinian stories of religion does not require the claim that the stories they suggest fail to provide an adequate explanation of either the payoff of religion or its mode of transmission. We will not attempt to show that these stories are not sufficient to explain the rise of religious belief and practice. One reason not to argue against the details of their stories is that both Dennett and Dawkins are very clear that they are providing a bare outline of what might be an adequate explanation. It would not be fair to try to score points by disputing the details they provide. The accounts they give are, as we said, speculations. A second reason not to dispute the details is that, for the purposes of our study, the more important issue is the use to which these stories can be put in the context of philosophical arguments. In other words, we are more interested in exploring the question, "So what?" Given the suggestions put forward by Dennett and Dawkins, what ought we conclude from the notion that there can be articulated a plausible Darwinian theory of religion? Because this question is the focus of our interest, it is not essential that we include every nuance and detail in the accounts given by Dawkins and Dennett. It is enough, then, that we have presented a fair summary of the central suggestions.

To begin to answer the "So what?" question, it would be helpful to look at what Dawkins and Dennett think we are supposed to learn from the adequacy of these stories. What conclusions do they suggest we ought to make? It turns out that they do not explicitly put forward any conclusions. They simply move on to other matters in their discussions of religion. This move is puzzling because they go to great lengths to articulate their suggestions. Dennett dedicates a whole section consisting of five chapters to "The Evolution of Religion" (95–246). Neither of them ever articulates an explicit claim that the fact that religious belief and practice can be explained in a Darwinian manner renders belief in God suspect. It is evident, however, that they believe that the presence of these explanations ought to make people less committed to their religious beliefs.

We want to make clear what the connections could be between the presence of Darwinian stories and the rationality of religious belief. There are at least four ways in which Darwinian stories can be employed in some kind of atheist worldview. The first two can be discussed briefly. The last two will require more development. While Dennett, at least, might implicitly embrace the third of the options, it is the fourth method that is more likely to capture the aims of both Dawkins and Dennett.

Two Benign Uses of Darwinian Stories

Darwinian stories could be put forward as an answer to the question, "Supposing that there is no God, how can we then account for the rise, distribution, and nature of religious belief and practice?" In this context, the Darwinian account is not put to polemical use. It is not explicitly a part of some argument against the existence of God. There is an element of disinterested curiosity about this approach. While theism can explain readily the disposition toward religious belief, a thinker might suppose that it is intriguing to explore the possible explanations that might fit with an atheistic view. Dawkins begins his discussion of the origin of religion with a statement reflecting this sort of approach: "Knowing that we are the products of Darwinian evolution, we should ask what pressure or pressures exerted by natural selection originally favoured the impulse to religion" (163).

While it might be tempting to think of this approach, or Dawkins' articulation of it, as being infected with a certain question begging, this criticism would be hasty. The Darwinian story can be put forward as the best account consistent with atheism for the widespread propensity to develop religious belief and practice throughout human history and culture. To use these stories in this way can be seen simply as a refinement or a filling out of the worldview of atheism. If atheism is true, then it has to have a plausible account for the major items we can observe in the natural world, human nature, and human culture. Since religion is one of these major items, it is fitting that atheists would develop their account.

The second use to which the Darwinian story of religion can be put is closely related to the first. A Darwinian account of religion can serve as an answer to a particular argument *against* atheism. Suppose a theist puts forward this question, "If there is no God, why are religious beliefs and practices so widespread?" The theist might articulate his argument in several ways. He could claim that there is no good atheistic explanation either for the near universality of religious belief or for the central role religion plays in the lives of the overwhelming majority of people in the world. Or he could argue, perhaps more plausibly, that the theistic explanation for these phenomena is a better explanation than any atheistic one.

Articulating a sophisticated Darwinian story of the rise and nature of religious belief and practice can be a good answer to such arguments. In fact, it amounts to a decisive refutation of the claim that there is no good atheistic explanation. It will also make the softer claim, that the theistic explanations are better, less convincing. This sort of theistic argument, then, can be undermined significantly by the Darwinian story of religion.

Darwinian Stories as Arguments for Atheism

There is a third use to which these stories might be put. An atheist can attempt to use the Darwinian story as part of an explicit argument against the existence of God. In this strategy, the possibility of a purely natural explanation of the rise and nature of religion is thought to show that there is no God or other supernatural being. Neither Dawkins nor Dennett explicitly adopts this strategy. In fact, Dennett seems to challenge it at one point.

> I might mean that religion is natural as opposed to *supernatural*, that it is a human phenomenon composed of events, organisms, objects, structures, patterns, and the like that all obey the laws of physics or biology, and hence do not involve miracles. And that *is* what I mean. Notice that it could be true that God exists, that God is indeed the intelligent, conscious, loving creator of us all and yet *still* religion itself, as a complex set of phenomena, is a perfectly natural phenomenon. (25; emphasis in original)

Dennett does not make this assertion in the context of his Darwinian stories, however. He is discussing what it means to take religion to be a natural phenomenon. Taking religion to be such, he says, is not incompatible with the existence of God. Presumably, then, he would think that the Darwinian story of religion is also not incompatible with the existence of God.

In his discussion of miracles, Dennett writes that the only way to show that a miracle occurred is by "adopting the scientific method, with its assumption of no miracles, and showing that science was utterly unable to account for the phenomena" (26). Only if science is utterly unable to account for something can we attribute it to a miracle. If the Darwinian story of religion provides a comprehensive explanation of religion, then science is not "utterly unable to account for the phenomena." It is, then, unreasonable to believe that there is some special act of God behind any religion. A Darwinian account of religion might be compatible with a deist God who never interferes in the universe he created, but it is not compatible with the sort of God that is concerned with human beings. Although Dennett does not explicitly endorse the idea that the presence of a Darwinian account of religion provides an argument that a theistic God (one who intervenes) does not exist, it does appear that he thinks such an argument can be strong. Because this strategy might lie behind Dennett's work, it is worth evaluating here the strength of the arguments that could be developed.

An argument against the existence of God based on the Darwinian story can be abbreviated as the following conditional statement:

(G): If there is a good Darwinian story of religion, the object of religion (a God who intervenes) probably does not exist.

Notice that what does the work in this argument summary is not the specific nature of the object in question. It is not because there is something special about God or about religion that the argument is thought to work. Rather, (G) is a particular instance of a general claim or principle:

(P): If there is a good Darwinian story of x, the object of $x(y)$ probably does not exist.

To see whether this principle is reliable, we can employ a parallel argument strategy, similar to the one employed as a criticism of the ontological argument for God's existence. We can plug different things into x and y and see where it gets us. Right away we hit a roadblock. Suppose we plug in *sense perception*, so the instance of (P) turns out to be

(S): If there is a good Darwinian story of sense perception, the object of sense perception (the physical world) probably does not exist.

There is a perfectly good Darwinian story of the rise and nature of sense perception. It does not seem that we ought to conclude that the world does not exist. There is something in the details of the Darwinian story of sense perception that is not found in the Darwinian story of religion, however. The physical world itself plays an essential role in the Darwinian story of sense perception. We could not develop a plausible Darwinian story of the origin of sense perception without assuming the reality of the physical world. In contrast, the reality of God does not seem to play an analogous role in the Darwinian story of religion. Therefore, the arguments are not exactly parallel.

We can solve this problem by revising our principle. Rather than using "(P): If there is a good Darwinian story of x, the object of x(y) probably does not exist," we ought to use a revised version of (P):

(RP): If there is a good Darwinian story of x, and the existence of the object of x(y) does not play an essential role in that story, then y probably does not exist.

This principle provides a better candidate to capture the parallel argument. It will help us distinguish cases where we think the inference might be strong, as in the case of religion, from cases in which we know it to be weak, as in the case of sense perception. The Darwinian argument against the existence of God can be formulated according to (RP) as follows:

(RG): If there is a good Darwinian story of religion, and the existence of the object of religion (a God who intervenes) does not play an essential role in that story, then a God who intervenes probably does not exist.

This formulation captures the revision of (P) and still applies to religious belief. The Darwinian story does not require God to exist in order to be plausible. The principle (RP), if true, would warrant the rejection of the existence of God.

What sort of instance might serve for a parallel argument? A good candidate will be found in the realm of mathematics. The truths of mathematics are thought by most mathematicians and philosophers of mathematics to be necessary truths. They are not simply empirical truths that depend on how things go in the universe. Nor are they conventional in that they could have been different depending on how human cultures developed. There are few mathematical relativists. The instance of (RP) dealing with mathematics will be

(M): If there is a good Darwinian story of mathematics, and the existence of the object of mathematics (necessary mathematical

truths) does not play an essential role in that story, then necessary mathematical truths probably do not exist.

To unpack this a bit more, the claim is that if there is a good
Darwinian account of the rise of mathematical belief and practice, as well as of its spread across cultures, and if this account
does not require the existence of necessary mathematical truths,
then we ought to conclude that such truths do not exist. The fact
that necessary mathematical truths exist, then, shows that there is
something wrong with this argument. If there is something wrong
with (M), then there is something wrong with (RG). Of course, it
is open to an objector to deny that (M) and (RG) are sufficiently
parallel. The objector, then, would have to explain in what ways
the instantiations are not parallel. It is possible, as well, to deny
the necessity of mathematical truths, although this is not a promising alternative.

There are other parallel arguments that show that the principle (RP) is false. The second example of an item for which there
can be a good Darwinian story is our belief that the laws of physics apply throughout the universe. This belief does not play an
essential role in the evolution of our ability to form beliefs and
practices conducive to physics (though it could be argued that
the belief that the laws of physics are constant across the history
and geography of earth or of Europe does play an essential role).
Another example is our belief in the general reliability of history
that transcends a few generations. We might be able to produce
a decent argument that the reliability of belief in recent history
(say, within two or three generations) aids survival. The reliability
of what we might call distant history, however, is not connected in
any way to the Darwinian story. We can develop a good Darwinian story of how our beliefs and practices about distant history
emerged. Ought we conclude that none of the claims of distant
history are true or that its methods are not truth conducive? It
seems not.

There is a fourth example that is more controversial. This is
the evolution of our moral beliefs and practices. We can, as both
Dawkins and Dennett do, come up with a good Darwinian story

about how these practices and beliefs emerge. Objective moral values or real moral obligations that are binding play no essential role in this story. While some thinkers will accept the consequent of this instance of (RP) and reject the existence of objective moral obligation, most will be hesitant. In chapter 3, we pointed out that Dawkins and Dennett seem to presuppose objective moral obligations in some of their own criticisms of religion. It is not open to them, therefore, to deny the reality of such obligations. The existence of these parallel arguments renders the conditional statement form (RP) suspect. If the statement form (RP) is faulty, then the instance (RG) does not provide the basis of a valid argument.

It is one thing to argue that something is wrong with an argument or principle. Is it another thing to identify exactly where the argument goes wrong. The problem with these arguments, in short, is that they extend the Darwinian stories beyond the scope of things that these stories set out to explain. A good Darwinian story can explain how human beings or human cultures come to have the capacities and tendencies they have. It cannot explain whether those capacities match up with anything in the world. In other words, it is the tendency of human beings to think mathematically or to have a moral sense or to develop religious rituals that is being explained. The existence of God, the necessity of mathematical truths, and the obligatory nature of moral truths lie outside the domain of what these stories aim to explain. Because of the limits of the scope of these arguments, they have nothing to say about the reality of God. It is this feature that Dennett was pointing out when he insisted that "it could be true that God exists, that God is indeed the intelligent, conscious, loving creator of us all and yet *still* religion itself, as a complex set of phenomena, is a perfectly natural phenomenon" (25; emphasis in original).

In summary, any argument from the presence of Darwinian stories of the rise and nature of religion to the claim that God does not exist will be on fairly weak ground. Again, it must be remembered, neither Dawkins nor Dennett explicitly endorses this sort of argument. Dennett seems implicitly to do so, and therefore, the possibility of using their stories in this way warrants our consideration. After investigating how such arguments might be developed, we can conclude that the availability of a Darwinian story of the rise of religious belief and practice does not count against the existence of God.

Darwinian Stories as Nietzschean Genealogies

There is another use to which the Darwinian stories might be put. These stories about the origin and nature of religious belief and practice can be put forward as a sort of Nietzschean genealogy. Nietzsche's use of genealogy is best developed in *On the Genealogy of Morality.*[4]

A genealogy is a story about origins. People often trace their genealogies in order to be able to show the rich or aristocratic heritage of their family name. Legitimation may come with a good genealogy. Nietzsche uses genealogy for another reason. He too wants to tell a story about origins, but his end is to show the poor and dirty origin of certain ideas that we often take to be high and mighty. His end is *delegitimation.* Normally, we criticize an idea by giving reasons against it. That is, we look for reasons to think the idea is false. Nietzsche is not looking for reasons to think the ideas of morality are false. Rather, he is looking for an explanation of how we come to have these ideas in the first place. How is it that we came to have the ideas of good and evil? This question is very different from the question of how it is that we justify our ideas of good and evil. According to Nietzsche, the story about how we got these ideas is a story about subrational or nonrational processes. The outcome of Nietzsche's discussion is that it seems plausible that morality does not come from God or from some fixed Platonic realm. Nor are moral concepts grounded in some universal necessary reason or some fixed human nature that is the essence of a person. Their origin is far more murky and illegitimate.

It is important to recognize that Nietzsche never argues that his genealogy is true. He does bring forth some etymological data as evidence, but he tells the story with a different purpose. He aims to dislodge our commitment to a moral point of view.

He wants to undermine our confidence that traditional moral claims are true. A Darwinian story about the rise and nature of religious belief and practice can be used in an analogous way to dislodge our commitment and confidence that religion offers a viable way of life. Both Nietzsche on the one hand and Dawkins and Dennett on the other hold forth stories that rival the traditional accounts of the nature of morality and religion, respectively.

There is some reason to think that both Dennett and Dawkins are employing a Nietzschean sort of strategy with their Darwinian stories. Three features of their approaches can lead one to make this claim. First, as we said, neither Dennett nor Dawkins claims that their Darwinian stories are true. As Dennett admits, "I am not claiming that this is what science has already established about religion. The main point of this book is to insist that we don't yet know—but we can discover—the answers to these important questions if we make a concerted effort" (103). What is held forth as a Darwinian explanation for the rise and nature of religious belief turns out to be speculative in a similar way that Nietzsche's genealogy is speculative. Second, the fact that Dawkins and Dennett do not draw any explicit conclusion from their Darwinian story supports the notion that they are employing the story for some purpose other than as a feature of a particular argument. It appears that they aim mostly to create an effect. The third reason to think that they may be employing a Nietzschean sort of genealogy is that the Darwinian story often does have exactly the same effect as the genealogy, and this effect is precisely the one that both Dawkins and Dennett aim to produce.

What makes the Nietzchean genealogical strategy effective is that it provides an alternative story that can undermine the reader's confidence in the traditional story. If Nietzsche (or Dawkins and Dennett) can get the reader to think that the alternative story just might be worthy of attention, or that something like this story just might be plausible, the reader's confidence in the legitimacy of his previous view of morality is undermined.

In this way the Darwinian story of the origin of religion can have the effect of dislodging the reader's confidence in the reality of God. As we saw when dealing with arguments based on the principle (RP), the existence of God is perfectly compatible with these Darwinian stories. They do not provide the basis for a good argument that God does not exist. A Darwinian story, taken as a Nietzschean genealogy, however, has rhetorical power to undermine confidence. Its efficacy is not connected to any real evidential value.

Remembering two facts will help us respond to the use of the Darwinian story as a genealogy. First, offering a speculative story or genealogy requires no commitment on the part of the one telling the story. Dawkins and Dennett can insist that they are merely suggesting the kinds of things that might eventually become well established. This posture is a relatively safe one, rhetorically speaking. They do not have to defend their suggestions, yet these suggestions can have the powerful psychological effect of undermining a reader's confidence in theism. If some particular Darwinian story is going to be taken seriously as a viable explanation for how religious beliefs and practices actually emerged, it must be defended as true and must be established the way other comparable theories are established.

Second, these Darwinian stories are genealogies clothed in the language of science. As such, their rhetorical power is far greater than that of other genealogies. It is easy for a reader to begin to assume that the meme-theoretic analysis of cultural items or the connection of religion with the principle that children obey what adults tell them has been established with the same rigor as the genetic theory of heredity, for example. This is not the case, as both Dawkins and Dennett rightfully emphasize. All of the details of these stories are speculative. To be sure, these details are worth pursuing with whatever research programs might be fruitful, but these speculations ought to carry little weight in evaluating whether theism is correct. The scientific-sounding context of this discussion can serve to make it more difficult for the readers to keep in mind the speculative nature of these suggestions. They have the trimmings of those advertisements for cars that use an actor in a scientist's lab coat to give the appearance of legitimacy.

The rhetorical power of these stories is far stronger than their evidential strength. The inherently nonrational mode of persuasion of the genealogical approach ought to remind us that it provides no real grounds to support the claim that there is no God.

Dennett and Dawkins each put forward rich Darwinian accounts of the origin and nature of religious belief and practice. While they do not articulate what follows from these accounts, we have looked at four uses to which such accounts can be put. Two of these uses are benign. They can serve as an explanation for religion on the assumption that atheism is true, and they can serve as a rebuttal to a specific argument for theism that could be put forward. The third use is to employ a Darwinian story of religion in an argument against the existence of God. We have seen that these arguments are not strong. The fourth use of the Darwinian account of religion is as part of a Nietzschean type of genealogy of religion. While such genealogies are rhetorically powerful, they ought not persuade us that belief in God is not reasonable.

CHAPTER SIX

Three Arguments for Atheism

Although the works of the New Atheists focus on different aspects of a total critique of religion, each one holds forth the claim that belief in God is rationally suspect. None of these books has as its main purpose to provide philosophical arguments for the claim that God does not exist. Along the way, however, each writer alludes to or develops various lines of reasoning or evidences for their atheistic claims. In this chapter, we shall investigate three of these arguments. Our aim is to find those arguments that have potential to play a significant role in the overall case against God. In the final chapter, we shall look at a fourth argument, the strongest argument for atheism that any of the writers presents.

Argument 1: Religious Pluralism Undermines the Rationality of Believing in God

In *Breaking the Spell*, Dennett raises the challenge that the wide variety of religious beliefs in the world counts against any particular religious truth claim. It is difficult, he thinks, for a religious believer to hold that his own religion is true while every other one is false. From Dennett's discussion, we can see that the tremendous plurality of religious beliefs raises three challenges to holding that any particular religion is true. The first challenge is that pluralism makes it impossible even to get a reasonable discussion started. Before we can begin to talk about God, Dennett raises the question, "Which God are we talking about?" (223). Before we can begin the discussion, he seems to think that we must show that all other concepts of God are faulty. In this way the plurality of religions undermines any attempt to make a case for the truth of any religious claim. "When it comes to God, on the other hand, there is no straightforward way of cutting through the fog of misunderstanding to arrive at a consensus about the topic under consideration" (217).

As we saw in chapter one, this challenge is easily overcome. It is possible to stipulate a concept of God for the purpose of investigation, and then to find reasons to think a being with this profile exists or does not exist. This procedure is, in fact, the one taken by Dennett when he characterizes religions as *"social systems whose participants avow belief in a supernatural agent or agents whose approval is to be sought"* (9; emphasis in original). As we observed in that chapter, if the approval of the supernatural agent or agents is to be sought, then there is reason to think that the agents have some concern about human beings. At least they have enough concern to approve or not. This characterization of religion, then, results in the beginning of a stipulation of a concept of God. We have seen that we can make progress in thinking about the case for or against God's existence before we have definitively rejected every religious conception except one.

The second challenge Dennett raises is that one who holds to the truth of one religion must have an account of why the other false religions exist. Dennett suggests that this question undermines the notion that there is any one religion that is true:

> Your religion, you may believe, came into existence when its fundamental truth was revealed by God to somebody, who then passed it along to others. It flourishes today because you and the others of your faith know that it is the truth, and God has blessed you and encouraged you to keep the faith. It is as simple as that, for you. And why do all the other religions exist? If those

people are just wrong, why don't their creeds crumble as readily as false ideas about farming or obsolete building practices? They will crumble in due course, you may think, leaving only true religion, your religion standing. (100–101)

These comments contain the sketch of an argument that no particular religion is true. The argument goes as follows:

(1) If one particular religion is true, the false religions will disappear.
(2) The false religions have not disappeared.
(3) Therefore, there is not one particular religion that is true.

Dennett allows that some religious believers might respond by predicting that the false religions *will eventually* crumble away. This response is a challenge to the second premise. It is to say that this premise, as it stands, is irrelevant. We ought not to expect the other religions already to have disappeared, but they will in due time. The believer who makes this move would revise the premise to read, "The false religions will disappear in the future." If this premise is true, this person might argue, the argument does not support its conclusion. Eventually the one true religion will be vindicated.

This response on the part of the theist is weak for several reasons. The first weakness is that there does not seem to be any evidence that the number of religions is decreasing. In fact, it seems to be increasing. Second, this response assumes that the first premise is essential to believing that there is a true religion. It is not the case that believing that one religion is true entails believing that the others will disappear. While Dennett is correct to say that there has to be an account for the existence of the various religions, this account does not have to include the claim that they will all disappear except for the true one.

A better response to Dennett's argument is to deny premise one. Not only is this claim not an essential part of the claim that one religion is true, but there are good religious reasons to think that this premise is false. If we assume that it is Christianity that is true, we will recognize that there are many religions that are mistaken about important issues. If they do not hold, for example, that Jesus is the unique Son of God, then they miss that aspect of the truth. Why are these religions still around? One answer could be that, even if they are not completely true, they are largely true. For example, Islam teaches that the most important things for human flourishing consist in being rightly related to the creator of the universe. This belief is held to be true by Christians. Buddhists think that our spiritual lives ought to be the foundation for our ethical lives. This claim is thought to be true by Christians as well. Many forms of Hinduism hold that this life is not all there is, and that what we do in this life affects our state in the next. What is shared by the various religions allows a person who is committed to the truth of one religion to affirm many of the important claims of other religions.

The third challenge that religious pluralism raises for one who thinks that there is a true religion is epistemological. With the plurality of religions, how can anyone have confidence that he has found the one that is true? Dennett points out the challenge:

> Whichever religion is yours, there are more people in the world who don't share it than who do, and it falls to you—to all of us, really—to explain why so many have gotten it wrong, and to explain how those who know (if there are any) have managed to get it right. Even if it is obvious to you, it isn't obvious to everyone, or even to most people. (92)

The reality of pluralism arises whenever a person holds something to be true. There are always a multitude of alternative claims for any topic. This challenge appears to be particularly acute when it comes to religion, however, because the methods of adjudicating religious claims are imprecise at best. Scientific practice tends to lead to a convergence of belief about the realms that are investigated. Religious practice does not. This lack of convergence leads many people to think that religious pluralism reveals that rational discussion of religion always reaches an impasse.

As we saw in both chapters 1 and 2, religious claims are not, for the most part, empirical claims subject to public confirmation. They are, rather, philosophical. They can be rationally evaluated through careful argumentation. The fact that there does not seem to be a growing convergence of belief shows that religious beliefs are similar to other nonempirical disciplines such as political theory, ethics, and, especially, metaphysics. The lack of convergence is similar in each of these domains of study.

In discussions of the challenges of religious pluralism, it is often overlooked that atheism is a position or a worldview as much as any religion is. There are two important aspects of this claim to consider. First, atheism makes its own set of claims, and these claims conflict with the claims of other worldviews. Just as a religious believer has to confront the reality that the majority of people do not share her views, the atheist also must recognize her position as holding views that are held only by a small minority of people. If we introduce this observation into Dennett's statement, this point would be made clear:

> *Whichever view about ultimate reality is yours,* there are more people in the world who don't share it than who do, and it falls to you—to all of us, really—to explain why so many have gotten it wrong, and to explain how those who know (if there are any) have managed to get it right. Even if it is obvious to you, it isn't obvious to everyone, or even to most people. (my paraphrase in italics)

If atheism is true, how is it that there are so few atheists? Part of what Dennett is attempting in his book is to provide an account of "why so many have gotten it wrong." (92) This task is fitting for an atheist confronting the plurality of worldviews. What we are challenging, here, is the idea that religious pluralism provides grounds to think that the religious people, in particular, *have* gotten it wrong.

A second point that is often neglected is that there is as much of a plurality within atheism as there is within religion. We discussed this point briefly in chapter 1. It is easy to think that atheism tracks the physical sciences and, since there is a convergence of belief in the sciences, there is little plurality in atheism. This assumption neglects the fact that atheism is a worldview, or a family of worldviews. What the members of this family have in common— perhaps the only thing they all have in common—is the denial of a supernatural agent. What the various atheistic worldviews differ about spans the entire range of philosophical opinions about any position. Some examples include whether objective moral obligations exist and, if so, how they are grounded; whether human beings have significant freedom of choice; whether properties such as colors are abstract objects; how it is that language connects with or reflects reality. These represent a very few of the topics in the discipline of philosophy about which atheists differ. Even questions about the fundamental forces in world affairs admit of deep differences among atheist thinkers. Some believe that all of the causal work in the universe can be explained in terms of the properties of molecular or submolecular particles. Others, such as the Marxists, think there are fundamental economic processes that are not reducible to chemistry yet which drive events. There are topics in many other disciplines such as political theory, aesthetics, sociology, and psychology where atheists differ with each other as well. The notion that there is a unified atheism, on the one hand, and a hopeless plurality of religions on the other is simply false.

The fact that atheism is itself a family of worldviews is often neglected because of a widespread assumption that atheism is neutral. In 1976, philosopher Anthony Flew published a book called *The Presumption of Atheism.*[1] Flew argued that "the debate about the existence of God should properly begin from the presumption of atheism, that the onus of proof must lie upon the theist" (13–14). Atheism, according to Flew, is not the positive claim that there is no such being as God. It is simply the lack of the belief in God. The view that there is a presumption of atheism results in the assumption that atheism is the neutral position. The theist is the one who must defend his claim. All the atheist must do is offer a critique of the evidence the theist puts forward. The atheist, on the other hand, needs no particular arguments to be rational as long as the theist did not make a strong case.

Atheism, as we have seen, is not a neutral position. It holds that certain things are true of reality. Furthermore, it sets parameters around what sort of explanations are going to be accepted. It is in as much need of evidence as any other worldview. Once we see that atheism is not neutral, and that subsequently there is no special burden of proof on the theist, we can see that religious pluralism does not count against the existence of God any more than it counts against atheism.

Argument 2: Who Made God?

We saw in chapter 3 that both Dawkins and Dennett raise the concern that God cannot serve as an adequate explanation for the universe or for life or for human beings because God would also require an explanation. The chain of explanations, then, cannot end in God. Dawkins makes this claim at numerous points throughout *The God Delusion*. It comes up in his critique of the cosmological argument when he claims that the arguments "make the entirely unwarranted assumption that God himself is immune to the regress" (77; see also 78, 109, 120–21, 143). We saw that Dennett also raises this concern as an objection to the cosmological argument: "Others prefer to accept the premise and then ask: What caused God? The reply that God is self-caused (somehow) raises the rebuttal: If something can be self-caused, why can't the universe as a whole be the thing that is self-caused?" (242). Hitchens weighs in on this argument as well, stating that "the postulate of a designer or creator only raises the unanswerable question of who designed the designer or created the creator. Religion and theology and theodicy . . . have consistently failed to overcome this objection" (71). In discussing the cosmological argument, we noted that the idea that God also requires a cause only counts against certain versions of the argument. These are versions that no philosopher or theologian has ever put forward.

Dawkins raises the concern about the cause of God not only in response to theistic arguments. He proposes that it makes up an independent argument against the existence of God:

> A designer God cannot be used to explain organized complexity because any God capable of designing anything would have to be complex enough to demand the same kind of explanation in his own right. God presents an infinite regress from which he cannot help us to escape. This argument, as I shall show in the next chapter, demonstrates that God, though not technically disprovable, is very very improbable indeed. (109)

The argument Dawkins offers can be articulated as follows:

(1) If God exists, God is a complex intelligent being.
(2) Any complex intelligent being requires an explanation outside of itself for its existence.
(3) Therefore, if God exists, he requires an explanation outside of himself for his existence.

It is not clear what Dawkins means by claiming that God would be complex. Certainly he does not mean that God is a complex physical thing made of different parts. He must mean that God's life requires a complex mental structure—albeit a nonphysical one. Does it follow from the claim that the structure of God's mental life is complex that God requires an external explanation? We will have to think about what requires an external explanation and what does not. This discussion will share features with our investigation of the cosmological and ontological arguments.

A complete explanation of most of the facts we encounter will appeal to other facts. In most cases, some of these other facts are external to the fact being explained and some are internal. Suppose we want to explain facts about a tree. For example, why is the tree where it is and why is it as tall as it is? Part of a complete explanation includes the fact that the acorn landed here and took root, and that the tree has been growing a long time. The fact that the acorn fell here, a long time ago, is an external fact. It is outside the thing we are trying to explain. That the tree is tall, however, is also explained in part by the nature of trees. That is what trees are and what they do. In the right conditions, they grow tall. So most explanations involve both external and internal facts.

Dawkins' argument claims that, if God exists, his existence is a fact that requires an external explanation. This claim can be challenged. In chapter 3 we saw that the ontological argument points to the idea that, if God exists at all, he exists necessarily. If the concept of God includes necessary existence, then, if he exists, he does not depend on any external fact for his existence. It is good to be reminded that there are other facts, as well, that are necessary and that do not require any external explanation. Mathematical facts are necessary in this way. The explanation for $1+1=2$ has to do with the nature of numbers, with the nature of addition, and the nature of identity. There are no external facts that are required to explain it. Most facts or truths we encounter, however, are contingent. Whether they are true is contingent upon the external facts. Is it the case that God, if he in fact exists, has the property of necessary existence?

There are two reasons to think that God, if he exists, exists necessarily. First, and less importantly, the history of thinking about the nature of God is nearly unanimous in thinking that God is a necessary being. Anselm is one thinker we discussed who held this claim. Augustine, Aquinas, and the majority of other thinkers did so as well. This historical fact does not show that the concept of God includes necessary existence, but it does show that the appeal to divine necessity is not an attempt to avoid some new challenging argument. This claim is part of the theological tradition.

The second reason to think that God exists necessarily is more important. When we say that some fact is contingent and needs at least some external explanation, we are saying that whether or not the fact obtains is, in some part, up to things outside it. So the location of the tree depends upon where the acorn is planted. The acorn could be planted in different places, and the location of the tree would be different in each case. The location of the tree is a contingent fact.

The laws of physics are also contingent in the same way. Consider, for example, inverse square law, that is, the fact that the force of gravity between two objects is proportional to one over the distance between two objects squared. This can be called a *global* fact because it does not depend on what happens in particular places in the universe the way facts about the tree depend upon local events. The inverse square law holds at every place in the universe. Even though it is a global fact, it is still a contingent fact. It is contingent upon the other laws of physics and the properties of physical objects. If the laws of physics or the properties of objects had been different in the right way, the inverse square law would not be true. If the universe worked such that an inverse cube law was true, in this case, the inverse square law would be false. So, despite the fact that a physical law is a global truth, it still may be contingent. It is at least logically or metaphysically possible that the laws of physics could turn out to be different than they in fact are.

Now suppose God exists and that he set up the laws of nature. They are contingent on the way God set them up. God himself is not subject to the laws of physics. What is it, then, on which God's existence could be dependent? His existence does not depend on any event or object within the universe. Nor does it depend upon how the universe works. It does not seem that there could be anything else on which he could depend. If there is nothing on which God's existence could depend, he exists necessarily, if he exists at all. The fact that he exists does not depend on anything outside him. It does not rely on any external explanation.

If God's existence is necessary, then Dawkins' argument fails. The second premise turns out to be false because there can be a complex intelligent being that does not require an explanation outside of itself for its existence. The question of the origin of God, then, does not generate a cogent argument against his existence. This criticism of Dawkins' argument does not require that the ontological argument be sound. The ontological argument makes an additional claim that it is metaphysically possible that a being with maximal greatness exists. Although a theist thinks it is possible (and that it is actual) that a being with maximal greatness exists, in order to rebut the "Who made God?" argument, he need only point out that the concept of God, whether possibly instantiated or not, includes necessary existence.

Argument 3: The Problem of Evil

The *problem of evil* is the name for a family of arguments from the existence or amount or distribution of evil in the world to the conclusion that God does not or probably does not exist. It is often considered to be the most serious challenge to the reasonability of belief in a God who is good, omnipotent, and omniscient. It is a bit surprising that the problem of evil does not play more of a role in the writings of the New Atheists. Each of them does argue that religious belief leads to behavior that is morally abhorrent. This argument about religious behavior plays a large role in the projects of both Hitchens and Harris. It does not amount to an argument against the existence of God, however. At best it could constitute a pragmatic argument against taking faith in God seriously or against taking people who believe in God seriously.

The charge that evil cannot be reconciled to God does get a brief treatment from Harris. Dawkins does not raise it because "it is an argument only against the existence of a good God. Goodness is no part of the *definition* of the God Hypothesis, merely a desirable add-on" (108; emphasis in original). Dennett hardly mentions it. He does include it as one of the arguments he thinks has diminishing returns. His pronouncement on the list is "I doubt that any breakthroughs are in the offing, from either side" (27). He also mentions, in a footnote, Alvin Plantinga's defense of religious belief in light of the problem of evil. He comments that the problem of evil "has recently been given a good rehearing in the wake of the tsunami in the Indian Ocean" (406–7n17). Hitchens does not articulate any version of the argument.

Harris raises the problem of evil specifically in view of the mechanism of evolution:

Biological truths are simply not commensurate with a designer God, or even a good one. The perverse wonder of evolution is this: the very mechanisms that create the incredible beauty and diversity of the living world guarantee monstrosity and death. The child born without limbs, the sightless fly, the vanished species—these are nothing else than Mother Nature caught in the act of throwing her clay. No perfect God could maintain such incongruities. It is worth remembering that if God created the world and all things in it, he created smallpox, plague, and filariasis. Any person who intentionally loosed such horrors upon the earth would be ground to dust for his crimes. (172)

He goes on to assert that there is no answer the theist can make to this argument:

The problem of vindicating an omnipotent and omniscient God in the face of evil (this is traditionally called the problem of theodicy) is insurmountable. Those who claim to have surmounted it, by recourse to notions of free will and other incoherencies, have merely heaped bad philosophy onto bad ethics. (173)

There are two major versions of the problem of evil. The first contends that the existence of evil is incompatible with the existence of God. This version can be called the *charge of contradiction*. The second is the claim that the amount or kind or distribution of evil is strong evidence against the existence of God. The *evidential argument*, as this version is known, grants that there is no logical contradiction between the existence of evil and the existence of God.

The charge of contradiction can be answered by arguing that it is possible that God has a good reason to allow the evil that he allows. Let us call a good reason to allow evil a *justifying reason*. If it is possible that God has a justifying reason, then it is possible that God can be good and allow evil to exist. If this scenario is possible, then there is no logical contradiction between the existence of God and the existence of evil. This strategy is often called the *free will defense* because free will is proposed as the main reason God might allow evil.[2] It would be better to call this response the *good reason defense* because it is not essential to the structure of the defense to appeal to human freedom.

Of course, if we begin to wonder whether God could have a justifying reason for evil, human freedom is one of the first items people raise. If human beings are free in the sense that what they choose is up to them and not inevitable in light of the events that occurred before they chose, then even an omnipotent God cannot allow us to remain free and determine the outcome of our actions. This kind of freedom is called *incompatibilist freedom* because, on this view, freedom is not compatible with determinism of any kind. If having incompatibilist freedom is a great good, then God has a reason to allow the possibility of evil. He grants us freedom because it is a great good, but he cannot guarantee the outcome of our choices (and allow those choices to remain free).

There are two major challenges here. First, is it the case that freedom is a great good? Second, is it reasonable to think that human beings have this kind of freedom? That human freedom is a great good is evident. Most of the things that make our lives worth living to us are connected with the freedom of the will. We will point out three. First, it is hard to make sense of the fact that a person can be morally responsible for her actions unless those actions are, in a significant way, up to her. Harris introduces this challenge only to reject later the claim that human beings have incompatibilist freedom. He observes that "either our wills are determined by prior causes, and we are not responsible for them, or they are the product of chance, and we are not responsible for them" (273). The relevant claim in this part of the discussion is that if our wills are determined, we are not responsible for them. In order to ground moral responsibility, it seems, we need our actions to be up to us.

Harris claims that human moral responsibility does not depend on incompatibilist freedom: "We can find secure foundations for ethics and the rule of law without succumbing to any obvious cognitive illusions" (272). The cognitive illusion he has in mind is the freedom of the will. Unfortunately, he does not explain how we can have a foundation for ethics without human freedom. There are some ways to make progress, but these are not open to Harris because, as we saw in chapter 3, he wants to defend the notion that there are objective moral obligations. If he were an error theorist, who claimed that moral statements are all false because there are no obligations, he could secure whatever is left of ethics without human freedom. He would also be able to secure a subjectivist ethic without human freedom. It is difficult to see how he can have real moral obligation without human freedom.

The second area of importance to our lives that is connected with substantial freedom is the arena of our personal projects and accomplishments. The fact that we choose to invest ourselves in causes, careers, or courses of study contributes to the value of these things to us. The experience of value is increased because we did not have to invest ourselves in these ways.

The third area is that of human relationships. The fact that we freely choose to enter into relationships increases their value. My wife's choice to love me, even after living with me for more than twenty-three years, makes her love for me one of the great goods in my life.

While these examples of how human freedom is a great good can be developed and defended in more detail, it is sufficient to recognize that many of the things that make our lives worth living to us are closely connected with freedom.

The second challenge to thinking that human freedom might be part of God's justifying reason to allow evil is the claim that human beings do not have the kind of freedom in question. Harris, in a long footnote, argues that the notion of the freedom of the will is not coherent (272–74n7). In a passage already cited, he sees what he thinks is an inescapable dichotomy in the concept of free will:

> It has long been obvious, however, that any description of the will in terms of causes and effects sets us sliding toward a moral and logical crevasse, for either our wills are determined by prior causes, and we are not responsible for them, or they are the product of chance, and we are not responsible for them. (273)

If our wills are determined by prior causes, then what we seem to choose is not up to us, after all. If our wills are not determined, then, Harris claims, they are a product of chance. In this case, as well, we are not responsible. The conclusion is that we do not have responsibility for our actions.

This argument, however, employs a false dichotomy: either our wills are determined or they are the product of chance. The two alternatives do not cover all of the alternatives. What ought to be claimed is this: either our wills are determined or they are not. If our wills are not determined, then it may be that they are the product of chance. There may be ways that our wills can be undetermined other than chance. One possibility is that human beings are agents in the sense that they have the capacity to initiate new causal chains without that initiation being caused by events outside of the person's conscious control. In this way, a human being can serve as the terminus of some causal regresses in the way that God is thought to serve as the terminus of other regresses in the cosmological argument. We often reveal that we have this kind of assumption about human action when we describe a series of events initiated by a person. For example, suppose a person breaks a window by throwing a rock at it. We can explain the series of events causally: "The window broke because the rock hit it in the right way. The rock hit it in the right way because it was traveling with the right trajectory and speed. The rock was traveling with the right trajectory and speed because Fred threw the rock. Fred threw the rock because he wanted to scare the skunk in his backyard." Notice that each step is an explanation by appeal to a cause except the last. When we get to the person's role in the series of events, we tend to shift from causal explanations to an explanation in terms of reasons. That is, we appeal to reasons that the person has for initiating the chain of events.

The fact that we explain events in this way does not prove that Fred is not caused to throw the rock wholly by the chemistry in his brain, which in turn is caused to be in that state by a chain of events that stretches back to the years before he was born. It may be possible that human action is wholly caused in this way, but we simply do not believe it. We explain human action by appeal to reasons as if we believe that the person evaluates the reason and chooses to act accordingly. If we thought that every human action was wholly causally explainable in terms of brain chemistry and muscle response, we would not appeal to the content of reasons as the explanation for behavior.

Some thinkers, Harris included, will be strongly reluctant to think of human beings as agents in this way. He writes that "[i]n physical terms, every action is clearly reducible to a totality of impersonal events merely propagating their influence . . ." (274). If Harris is correct, then there is no human freedom of the incompatibilist sort we are defending. There is a good reason to think, however, that Harris is mistaken about human beings. If Harris' statement is true, then the reason he typed this particular sentence has nothing to do with the fact that he believes that the sentence represents accurately a fact about human beings. It has to do only with chemical reactions in his brain and the events that caused those reactions. Harris claims that the reason he types this or any other sentence is clearly reducible to impersonal events— events that have no cognitive content. If he is correct, it would be merely a lucky accident that any sentence he typed turned out to be true. Yet Harris wants us to believe that this sentence is true and that he has good reasons to think that it is true. He cannot have it both ways.

Harris has not shown that the freedom of the will is incoherent. In fact, he has set himself up for some criticisms that look, on the face of it, devastating to his case against God. Since the freedom of the will is coherent, the connection of free will and moral responsibility gives us good reason to think that human beings are significantly free. In this case, then, human freedom can be a justifying reason for God to allow evil. The existence of evil does not contradict the existence of God.

Of course the charge of contradiction is only one version of the problem of evil. The more difficult argument to challenge is the evidential argument from evil. Given that God could have a justifying reason to allow evil, it still does not seem likely that he has a reason to allow each case of evil that we encounter. The most influential version of the evidential argument comes from William Rowe.[3] He argues that if there is a case of evil such that God could have no justifying reason to allow it, then God does not exist. Considering the evils in the world gives us reason to think that it is unlikely that God has a justifying reason for allowing every case of evil. We can capture his reasoning as follows:[4]

(1) It *seems* as though there is no justifying reason for God to allow some particular evil.

(2) Therefore, it is *probably true* that there is no justifying reason for God to allow some particular evil.

If (2) is true, then it is probably true that there is no God. At first glance, this reasoning appears to be strong. After all, if we search for a justifying reason long enough, and we come up empty, we can begin to think that it is more likely that there is no justifying reason for the evil in question.

We can challenge Rowe's case, however. We can argue that Rowe's grounds are insufficient for thinking that it is probably true that there is no justifying reason for God to allow the particular evil.[5] The inference from the claim that it *seems* as though there is no justifying reason to be found to the conclusion that it is *probably* the case that there is no justifying reason turns out to be a weak inference. To support this criticism, let us consider what kind of inference we are asked to make here. The general form is, *It seems as though there is no x, therefore, probably there is no x.* Sometimes this kind of inference is a strong inference and sometimes it is not. Consider the following instantiation: *It seems as though there is no live elephant in this room, therefore, probably there is no live elephant in this room.* This is a good inference. It is perfectly reasonable to look around the room and say, "It seems as though there are no live elephants here, so probably there aren't any." Consider, however, the following instantiation: *It seems as though there is no carbon-14 atom in the room, therefore, probably there is no carbon-14 atom in the room.* This inference is fairly weak. The difference between an instantiation that yields a strong inference and one that yields a weak one turns on how reasonable it is for us to expect that we would detect the presence of whatever it is that we substitute for x. We get a strong inference when the same substitution makes the following sentence true: *If there were an x, we would probably know it.* Replacing x with *live elephant* results in a true sentence. When we replace x with *carbon-14 atom*, we get a false one. Even if there were carbon-14 atoms in the room, we would have no way of detecting them.

To see how strong the evidential argument for evil is, we must try to determine whether a reason that would justify God for allowing a particular instance of evil is more like an elephant or more like a carbon-14 atom. Is it more reasonable to believe that we would be able to figure it out if it is there or that we would not be able to figure it out? Consider whether the following sentence is true: *If God had a justifying reason to allow the particular case of evil, we would probably know what it is.* How likely is it that we should know what his reasons are? It is reasonable to think we should expect to be able to discern some likely candidates in some cases but not in others. No one thinks that we should be able to figure out God's reasons in every case. By the same token, no one will argue that we cannot discern what his reasons very well could be in many cases. Where disagreement remains about the evidential argument is in the degree to which we ought to expect to discern more justifying reasons than we can. Those who press the argument against God's existence overestimate the percentage of cases in which we ought to be able to figure all of this out, and they underestimate the percentage of cases in which we actually can.

Let us call some particular evil *mysterious* if the following is true of it. First, after some careful reflection, we have no idea how any of the standard repertoire of reasons that might justify God to allow some evils apply to this particular evil event. For example, we cannot see how preserving the freedom of the will, or preserving the regularity of cause and effect, or any other potential reason is relevant to the evil in question. Second, we cannot think of any additional reasons (beyond the standard ones) that might justify God in allowing this evil. A case of evil that satisfies both of these conditions is mysterious. All other cases of evil, then, we could call *nonmysterious*.

It is important to note that for an evil to count as nonmysterious, it is not necessary that we know what God's reasons actually are for allowing it. We only need to see that it is not clear that certain reasons do not apply to it. The reason this last caveat is critical is that we are trying to determine not what God's reasons are but whether it is reasonable to think that there are reasons available that would justify God in allowing the evil. If some particular evil is nonmysterious, then we have some idea that some potential reason we know about just might apply to it.

Most of the evils in the world fall into the category of the nonmysterious. It is only a small percentage of the evil things in the world that are such that we have no idea what kind of reasons might apply. For the mysterious evil, we ask the question, "If God has sufficient reason to allow it, would we expect to be able to discern what it is?" The answer is that we ought not expect to be able to discern his reasons. If God exists, we would expect that there would be significant stretches of reality that are beyond our grasp. We would expect that some of what is beyond our grasp would have to do with God's reasons for doing and allowing the things he does. The fact that there is mysterious evil is just what we would expect if there were a God. We ought to expect some significant mystery about his particular purposes, especially in the darkest times of our lives. If this is about what we should expect, it cannot be counted as evidence against God's existence. So even though it might seem, at first glance, that there are no good reasons to allow certain evils we see, this does not provide strong evidence that these evils are really unjustified. The evidential argument from evil, then, does not make it likely that God does not exist.[6]

In this chapter we investigated three of the arguments against the existence of God that are put forward by the New Atheists. Each one was found to be significantly flawed. Thus far, their case against God is not strong. In the final chapter, we will engage what we believe is the strongest argument against the existence of God they offer. It is an argument from Dawkins that the world as we find it fits better with the atheistic hypothesis than it does with the theistic hypothesis.

CHAPTER SEVEN

The Fittingness Argument

In the previous chapter, we discussed a variety of arguments against the existence of God that are laced throughout the work of the New Atheists. None of the arguments were found to be very strong. In this chapter, we will turn our attention to the strongest argument against the existence of God that any of these authors has put forward. This argument is one offered by Dawkins.

Dawkins' argument is built on the claim that a universe made by God would be different than one that is a product only of natural processes. This claim is part of Dawkins' insistence that religious beliefs should be treated as scientific hypotheses. That is, God's existence ought to make some difference to the world that is detectable. He claims, "A universe with a creative superintendent would be a very different kind of universe from one without" (55). If God's existence made no difference at all to what we observe about the universe, we would wonder to what belief in God amounted.

Given that a theistic universe should be different from an atheistic one, which does our universe look like? Dawkins claims that our universe fits well within the parameters of an atheistic worldview. It is quite different, he insists, than what fits with the view that God exists. Our observations about the world show us that it has the marks of an atheistic universe rather than the marks of a theistic one. We can sketch Dawkins' argument as follows:

(1) A theistic universe (one made by God) would be different than an atheistic universe (one that came about by only natural occurrences).

(2) Our universe fits better with an atheistic universe than with a theistic universe.

(3) Therefore, our universe is more likely to be an atheistic universe than it is to be a theistic universe.

Before we interact with this argument, it will be helpful to make some preliminary observations. First, why think this argument is the best one offered? Which argument is best will be a matter of some disagreement among those who engage with the work of the New Atheists. This argument can be counted as the best that is offered because it does support the conclusion to a degree. Two of the three arguments discussed in the last chapter were flawed in fairly obvious ways. The problem of evil can present a challenging argument, but none of the New Atheists develop it in ways that are not easily answered. This argument is much stronger. There are aspects of the universe as we know it that do fit better with an atheistic worldview than with a theistic worldview, and these aspects do raise the likelihood that atheism is true.

The second observation is that this argument does not aim to prove that God does not exist. Rather it aims to show that it is more likely that God does not exist than that he does. It is an evidential argument. The evidential nature of the argument is another one of its strengths. Dawkins is right when he insists, in many places throughout his book, that he is not providing a watertight proof that God does not exist. As we saw in chapter 2, it has become something of a slogan that one cannot prove God's existence or nonexistence.

As we have mentioned, philosophical disputes are both evidential in nature and cumulative. In investigating the case for some philosophical claim such as the existence of God, we take all of the evidential arguments together and try to determine in which direction the total case points. Some arguments or lines of evidence point in one direction, while others point in the opposite direction. The cumulative nature of arguments is common throughout the disciplines as well. There is rarely one line of argument that by itself establishes some significant claim with a high degree of confirmation. Dawkins is right to develop this argument along evidential lines in this way.

Third, this argument is one about *fittingness*. The argument claims that ours is the sort of universe that fits better with the view that there is no God. It also claims that the universe as we find it does not fit as well with the existence of God. In this way, we can test our two worldviews. We can figure out what sort of universe best fits with each, and we can look and see through empirical and other means whether the nature of the universe fits better with one theory or the other.

It is important to clarify the notion of fittingness that is at work. The issue of whether some observation fits or does not fit with a claim or a theory can be called an issue of *connectedness*. Connectedness comes in degrees. An observation connects more or less well with the theory or claim in question. There is little precision here, but we can recognize different general levels of connectedness and, consequently, different strengths of connectedness claims. For example, to say that some theory requires that a claim be true (or that some fact requires that a certain theory be true) is a tight level of connectedness. We can find such a tight level positively or negatively. The charge of contradiction discussed in the previous chapter is a claim that the existence of God requires that the universe have no evil in it at all. That a theory requires some claim to be true is the highest level of connectedness that can be proposed. A requirement claim, then, is a strong one and, as we saw, not difficult to refute.

A moderate level of connectedness involves expectations. Any theory leads us to expect certain things to hold and other things not to hold. These things may not be required (such that their not holding is incompatible with the theory), but the expectation can be strong. For example, if theism is true, we would expect there to be some connection between the purposes of God and the purposes for human existence. Such a connection is probably not required by theism but we would expect it. One indication that a feature is to be expected is if the lack of that feature would be at all surprising given the truth of the theory. The fact that it would be surprising if there were no connections between the purposes for human existence and God's purposes gives us reason to think that we should expect there to be a connection.

There is a level of connectedness that is even less tight than expectation. This is the level on which Dawkins' argument trades on. It is the level of *fittingness*. Certain observations fit better with one theory than with another, even if the theory would not lead us to expect the details of the observation. Fittingness is the sort of connectedness that is often appealed to in human interaction. You may have no reason to expect to see me in Starbucks, but it certainly fits with what you know about me (if you know anything about me at all).

These distinctions are important because there is a little danger of assuming that we know what to expect if atheism were true or if theism were true. For example, it is too strong to claim that if atheism is true, we would expect complex life to emerge via a long process something like natural selection. On the assumption that atheism were true, we would not expect there to be complex life at all. Given that there is complex life of the sorts we observe, perhaps the most we can claim is that the development of life by a process like natural selection fits better with atheism than it does with theism. (This is exactly how Dawkins' argument is put forward.) So too on the theistic theory, we might not expect that God would create conscious beings because we have little ground to know what to expect. That there are conscious beings very well may fit better with the theistic view, or so it will be argued.

The advantage of taking Dawkins' argument as one concerning fittingness rather than expectation is that the argument is for a weaker claim. If he is putting forward a weaker claim, it is more difficult to challenge it. It is not difficult to raise objections to strong claims (such as that evil is incompatible with theism). One only has to undermine the strong connection. A weaker claim, however, is more difficult to challenge. So, the fact that Dawkins claims that our universe fits better with atheism than it does with theism makes this argument stronger.

Having explained some important background observations, we can turn to the argument itself. Each of the two premises must be investigated. If both are true, then the argument works and the conclusion is established. The first premise is the claim that a universe made by God would be different than one made by natural occurrences. To evaluate this claim we must do a little clarifying work first. It is obvious that a universe made by God is different than one not so made in virtue of its having been made intentionally by a supernatural being. This sort of difference is not sufficient to get the argument going. If the argument is to progress, the difference between the theistic universe and the atheistic universe must be a detectible difference. It is in this way that Dawkins claims that the existence of God is to be treated as a scientific hypothesis. It is a claim that has, he thinks, detectible implications.

We will not dispute this claim here. In chapter 1, we discussed NOMA (the view that science and religion are Non-Overlapping Magisteria). We agreed with both Dawkins' and Dennett's rejection of this view of the relationship between science and religion. Some scientific and religious claims may overlap. Therefore, Dawkins is right in his claim that the sort of universe that fits with God's existence should be different in detectible ways than the sort of universe that fits with atheism.

If the argument proceeds from the claim that a theistic universe differs in detectible ways from an atheistic universe, we ought to think about what makes something detectible. Dawkins is disposed to think of detectability in terms of sense experience and the methods of the natural sciences. Something that is detectible is in principle subject to scientific investigation. The sorts of observations on which they reflect, then, tend to be empirical observations. It may be, however, that other sorts of observations can show us that there is a detectible difference between theories.

For example, it seems reasonable that ethical theories can differ from each other in detectible ways. If one theory prohibits lying in every circumstance while a second theory allows lying under specified conditions, there is a detectible difference between them. This is not the sort of detectible difference that decisively falsifies one of the theories. We would need to have a sense already that lying is permitted in some circumstances (or that it is never permitted) in order to use this difference to choose between theories. This detectible difference between the theories is not an empirical difference. The difference is due to the sort of moral assessment that each theory supports.

Given that there ought to be detectible differences between the claim that the universe is theistic and the claim that it is not theistic, even if some of these differences do not have to be empirically detectible, we can grant that the first premise of the argument is true. It remains to investigate the second premise. Does the universe as we observe it fit better with the theistic story than it does with the atheistic story? We must make careful observations to see whether there are good reasons to think that the second premise is true.

Although Dawkins does not spell out the way our universe fits with atheism precisely, he does point in the direction of what he has in mind. His view is that any naturalistic universe with complex life would include a long period of biological development through a process something like natural selection. This notion is built into his articulation of the naturalistic worldview that is an alternative to the God hypothesis. He states that "any creative intelligence, of sufficient complexity to design anything, comes into existence only as the end product of an extended process of gradual evolution" (31). Furthermore, he holds that a theistic universe would most likely not include a long process of biological development. He does not make this claim explicitly in connection with this argument, but it seems to lie behind his approach. In this case, his argument is that natural selection does not fit well in a theistic universe, but it fits neatly in a naturalistic universe. Since the evidence that life developed through natural selection is overwhelming, the probability that the universe is naturalistic is very high.

To what degree does biological development through natural selection fail to fit neatly with a theistic universe? There is a degree to which it does run counter to theism. In a theistic universe, the origin of various life forms is not restricted to processes that are gradual. God could use any process he wants to create living things. It is perfectly possible, if God exists, that he just brings living things into existence in all their variety at one moment. He is not restricted to processes that run over long periods of time. In this way our expectations about the development of biological life in a theistic universe ought to be wide open. Theism does not rule out a long process of biological development, but theists are not restricted to such theories by their theistic commitments.

An atheistic universe, in contrast, lacks the resources for instantaneous creation of all life forms. It would be completely baffling if complex life emerged instantly in a universe without God. Complex life would require some kind of long developmental process. This process would not need to be through genetic variation and natural selection, but it would need to be gradual. It would need to be, it turns out, something very like the way we find it.

Since the theistic universe is compatible with a variety of mechanisms for the development of complex biological life, the fact of gradual development through natural selection does not provide specific evidence for theism. Since the naturalistic universe seems to require some kind of long-term biological process for complex biological life, the fact of natural selection does confirm the naturalistic universe. This aspect of the universe we find, then, does support the claim that there is no God. It is important that we recognize that natural selection provides evidence for atheism even though it is the case that it is not incompatible with theism.

That natural selection lends evidence to the claim that the universe is naturalistic is part of what makes this argument the best one Dawkins offers. If all we look at is the development of complex biological life, his case would be quite strong. Other aspects of the universe as we find it, however, point in the opposite direction. There are at least four major elements of our universe that fit significantly better with a universe in which God exists than with the atheistic universe. These elements are the fact that the universe is ordered and susceptible to rational investigation, that it is a world with consciousness, that it is a world with significant free agency, and that it is a world with objective moral obligations. Each of these aspects fits neatly into a theistic world but is not at home in a naturalistic world. It is not that they are incompatible with naturalism, but they do not fit neatly into the naturalistic world.

It is important to be very clear about the structure of the argument being developed here. It is not an argument that moves directly from these four features of the world to the claim that God exists. It is a parallel argument structured in a way that is strongly analogous to Dawkins' argument. Gradual development of complex life through natural selection is something that fits better with atheism than with theism. This fact, as a result, supports the claim that God does not exist. Features of the world that fit better with theism than with atheism will support the claim that God does exist. If the arguments are strongly analogous, and these features do fit better with theism, then either Dawkins' argument is not very strong after all, or the universe as we find it points more clearly in the direction of theism than it does atheism.

A World That Is Ordered and Susceptible to Rational Investigation Fits Better in a Theistic Universe

If God exists, the universe is the product of purposeful action. It is made by an intelligent mind for reasons. The fact that the universe is made by a mind for reasons leads us to expect that it will be something that can be grasped rationally. It makes sense that there would be stable laws that allow predictions to be made and inferences to be drawn. It is not merely the case that an ordered universe fits better with theism; the level of connectedness is stronger than that. An ordered universe is what we would expect if God exists. If God exists and made the universe for reasons, it would be surprising if that universe exhibited none of the order that would make it susceptible to rational investigation. If it would be surprising that it would not be ordered, then its being ordered is something we would expect on the view that God exists.

A naturalistic universe, however, would not have to be susceptible to rational investigation. It fits perfectly well with a naturalistic universe that it be wildly chaotic. We saw in chapter 4 that the odds of a universe with heavy elements and a stable structure emerging without design are quite small. These elements are the minimum necessary for a universe to be subject to rational investigation. Of course, being susceptible to rational investigation is not incompatible with a universe without God, but the theory that God does not exist allows the universe to exhibit any one of a wide variety of descriptions as far as order is concerned. The fact that our universe is in fact ordered and susceptible to investigation is what we would expect if God does exist.

A World with Consciousness Fits Better in a Theistic Universe

Human consciousness involves several features that are difficult to fit with naturalism. Two of these features are the first-person experience and the intentionality of some of our mental states.[1] The first-person experience is illustrated by the fact that each person owns his own mental states. More importantly, we seem to have a special kind of access to our own mental states. For example, we never walk into a room and say, "There is a bad headache in this room. I wonder if it is mine." If someone has a bad headache, he knows that he does. He knows it in a way that other people cannot. Each person has privileged access to his own headache. In the same way, a person knows that she is thinking about coffee at a particular time. She may not know what someone else is thinking about. Our access to other people's thoughts is indirect. We can tell someone that we are thinking about coffee, or people can deduce it from our behavior or our habits, but we can know our own thoughts directly.[2] There is an ownership of our first-person perspective.

The intentionality of mental states involves the feature that our thoughts represent or are about things in the world, things in the past, and even things that do not exist. So right now, we can think about Niagara Falls, even though it may be hundreds of miles from where we are. We can think about Pickett's charge in the battle of Gettysburg, even though it occurred over 140 years ago. We can think about whether Santa Claus has any children, even though there is no Santa Claus. How is it that something inside me, my mental states, can be about something outside of me? This is the puzzle of intentionality.

Intentionality sometimes does not seem mysterious to us because we are language users. Noises articulated by a person or marks on a paper also can be about things in the world. That a string of marks such as "There is a hot cup of coffee in the kitchen" can express (truly or falsely) a fact about the world is due, however, to the prior activity of conscious minds. We assign meaning to language. Its meaning, then, is derivative. Particular strings of marks or articulate noises are meaningful because of the conventions of communities of conscious minds. Explaining how the English word *coffee* came to refer to the drink is an interesting and complicated story. Behind such stories always lie various communities of conscious beings. Their thoughts do much of the work in explaining how certain words came to pick out certain items. Figuring out how human minds can think of objects is more complicated still. Both the first-person perspective and the intentionality of mental states are some of the challenges for contemporary philosophy of mind.[3]

If God exists, then the primary thing that exists is itself a conscious mind of unlimited power and intellect. This mind has its own first-person perspective, and it can think about things. The notion that such a mind, if it creates anything, would create other conscious minds that have their own first-person perspectives and can think about things is not a great mystery. Is the existence of created conscious beings something that we ought to expect if theism is true? We ought to be cautious here.[4] We could develop an argument that consciousness is a good thing and a God who is good would have reason to create other conscious beings. If this line of thought is strong, then we would have reason to expect other conscious beings to exist if God does. We do not need to insist on this argument, however. All we need is to argue that the existence of conscious minds fits better with theism than with the view that the universe is naturalistic.

The view that there is no God, especially on Dawkins' version, includes the claim that any complicated living things that exist are the product of a long natural process of development from simpler living things. On this view, any species that contains animals with conscious minds originates ultimately from species that have no conscious minds by processes that are not executed by any conscious mind. If atheism is true, it is somewhat unusual that there would be any conscious minds.

We do not need to insist that any naturalistic theory of consciousness will be less than plausible.[5] Rather, this argument is that the phenomenon of consciousness is not something that fits easily into a naturalistic world. The attempt to explain consciousness within the parameters of naturalism has been designated the *hard problem* of consciousness.[6] The difficulty is indicative of, among other things, the lack of fit between atheism and the existence of conscious beings. The existence of conscious beings, like the order of the universe, is a detectible feature of the universe that fits better with theism than with atheism.

A World with Significant Free Agency Fits Better in a Theistic Universe

As we saw in the last chapter, many philosophers believe two things about human freedom. They believe that if an act is determined in any way, it cannot be free, and they believe that human beings have a significant degree of freedom. They are incompatibilists and libertarians. Freedom is not compatible with determinism, and we do have some significant freedom. Other philosophers are incompatibilists but not libertarians. They believe that freedom and determinism are not compatible but that we are not free in the relevant sense. Such philosophers are often called hard determinists.[7] It appears that Harris fits into this category (see Harris, 272–74). Still others (perhaps the majority) are compatibilists of one sort or another. They believe that an action can be both determined and free. We own our actions in a manner sufficient to guarantee that we are responsible for them, even if they are caused ultimately by events outside our control.[8]

Those philosophers who are libertarians generally think that the kind of freedom that could be compatible with determinism is not sufficient to ground moral responsibility. In addition, they point to our experience of choosing as a reason to believe that certain choices are up to us in this more robust sense. If the libertarians are right, then not everything about human beings is causally determined. Thus the world of people is not a causally closed world. As we discussed in the previous chapter, it is possible to defend this view of freedom against the challenges of thinkers such as Harris.

If human beings are free in this sense, then this fact is another feature of the universe that fits much better with theism than it does with atheism. In a naturalistic universe that is ordered enough to have complex life, we would expect events to proceed from previous events. Whether this universe would be determined or not, we would not expect the sort of beings that can purposely initiate actions that result in new chains of events. Yet this is the sort of agency we seem to have. That there are persons with libertarian agency does not seem to fit if the universe is naturalistic.[9]

If God exists, however, he acts for reasons. He chooses, among other things, to create the universe, the plants and animals, and to create other minds. He creates these things because he wants to do so. He did not have to do so. He causes them to come into existence. He is not constrained to do so by factors outside himself. God himself is free in a libertarian sense. It is not mysterious that God would create beings that are free in the same sense. The primary thing that exists in the theistic universe is a being with libertarian agency. That we find ourselves with this sort of freedom, then, is something that fits well into the theistic story. The connection between a theistic universe and the existence of other agents who are free in a libertarian sense may even be stronger. If God's reasons to create human beings include his purposes for their moral and spiritual development, the existence of libertarian freedom is even more to be expected.

A World with Objective Moral Obligations Fits Better in a Theistic Universe

It seems clear that there are moral obligations that are objective in the sense that they hold whether or not one wants them to hold or one wants to fulfill them. A claim such as "It is wrong to torture a person to death for no particular reason" seems to be true, and the obligation it prescribes seems to be binding on all human beings. It is hard, after all, to imagine that such an obligation is binding only because of the desires or goals of some individual person or of some society. It is, then, at least reasonable to think that objective moral obligations exist. We noted in chapter 3 that Harris explicitly defends objective obligations and that it seems that the other New Atheists presuppose objective obligations in their criticism of the immoral behavior of religious people and institutions.

If there are such obligations, they make up another detectible feature of the universe that does not fit well within a naturalistic worldview. In chapter 3, we looked at an argument for the existence of God from the existence of moral obligations. We saw that versions of this argument can be fairly strong. There we cited John Mackie as admitting that objective moral obligations "make the existence of a god more probable than it would have been without them."[10] We also discussed George Mavrodes' claim that the kind of moral obligations we find in the world are not at home in an atheistic universe. Even if these arguments do not show that God exists, they serve to support the claim we are making here, that moral obligations fit better in a theistic world than in an atheistic world.

If God invented human beings, he did so for a reason or reasons. Some of these reasons may ground moral obligations. For example, if God made us with moral ends in mind—if he made us so that we would embody certain virtues, for example—his setting up moral reality the way he did makes a good deal of sense. If God has spiritual purposes for us—that we would find a relationship with him and experience him as our highest good—he may set up moral rules as guidelines for how best to do that. Whatever God's purposes are, it makes sense that he would make us the kinds of beings that are subject to moral truths and that can understand and act on them.

Paul Draper is an agnostic philosopher who made a similar point: "A moral world is, however, very probable on theism."[11] In other words, if theism is true, we ought to expect a moral world, that is, a world with objective moral obligations. In contrast, such obligations do not fit as well in an atheistic world.

We are now in a position to sum up Dawkins' argument in light of the details of our response. Dawkins' strongest argument against the existence of God goes as follows:

(1) A theistic universe (one made by God) would be different than an atheistic universe (one that came about by only natural occurrences).

(2) Our universe fits better with an atheistic universe than with a theistic universe.

(3) Therefore, our universe is more likely to be an atheistic universe than it is to be a theistic universe.

The main work in this argument is done by the second premise, that our universe fits better with an atheistic universe than it does with a theistic universe. The detectible feature Dawkins points to as an indication of this better fit is the development of complex life over a long period of time through natural selection. In a universe with no God but with complex life, we would expect there to have been a long process of development. The fact that life did develop in this way, then, lends confirmation to the atheistic hypothesis. One virtue of Dawkins' best argument, then, is that it does identify one way in which the universe that we observe points to the conclusion that no God exists. We have identified, however, four other detectible features of our universe that may be relevant to premise two of the argument. Each of these four features fits better with a theistic universe than it does with an atheistic universe.

Many philosophers have developed theories to show that these features of the universe are compatible with a naturalistic worldview. Some of these strategies might succeed. Even if these attempts are successful, they do not undermine the strength of these criticisms of Dawkins' argument. These criticisms do not depend on the lack of good naturalistic explanations for these features. Regardless of the availability of naturalistic explanations, it remains the case that these features still fit better with the view that God exists.

In the interest of clarity, it is worth reiterating the nature of our strategy here. We have not put forward an argument from these four features of the universe to the claim that God, in fact, exists. Fairly strong arguments of this kind can be developed, but it is beyond the scope of this book to do so. The four features we identify show that there is good reason to reject the second premise of Dawkins' argument. Either this premise is not true or, at the very least, Dawkins has not given us very strong reasons to think that it is true. Therefore, the argument he presents turns out to be not well supported. There are too many detectible features in our world that simply do not fit well with atheism. Dawkins' best argument does not, in the end, deliver.

≡

A Modest Conclusion

The writings of the New Atheists are marked with excitement and rhetorical power. The public response, both in their favor and in opposition to them, has been impassioned as well. One conclusion is beyond dispute: people care deeply about religious questions. The aim of this present book is to take a cooler, more reflective approach in engaging the nature of the case they offer for the truth of atheism. As we have seen, this case is multifaceted. The New Atheists present and allude to a variety of arguments that God does not exist or that belief in God is rationally suspect. We looked at their views concerning faith and reason, and science and religion, and we engaged their criticisms of theistic arguments. None of their challenges were found to be decisive. In chapter 5, we explored Darwinian stories of the emergence of religious belief. We concluded that, although such stories can be psychologically effective in dislodging a reader's commitment to her religious beliefs, they do not undermine the reasonability of belief in God. In chapter 6, we discussed three of the main arguments against the existence of God that are raised by the New Atheists. These arguments were each found not to be persuasive. In chapter 7, we discussed the strongest argument they have to offer. Although Dawkins does identify one feature of the universe that does fit better with atheism than theism, the overall argument is not strong. The universe as we observe it points more clearly in the direction of theism.

Despite the eloquent writings of the New Atheists, we are left with the conclusion that the case against God as presented is not strong enough to worry someone who already believes in God. Nor should their arguments persuade one who considers belief in God for the first time. The God of traditional religions survives the sustained argument against his existence. Although we have not presented a total case for God's existence, we have laid a secure enough foundation to be confident that belief in God is belief in a *Reasonable God*.

Notes

Introduction

1 Sam Harris, *The End of Faith: Religion, Terror, and the Future of Reason* (New York: Norton, 2004); Daniel Dennett, *Breaking the Spell: Religion as a Natural Phenomenon* (New York: Viking, 2006); Richard Dawkins, *The God Delusion* (Boston: Houghton Mifflin, 2006); and Christopher Hitchens, *god is not Great: How Religion Poisons Everything* (New York: Twelve Publishers, 2007). Unless otherwise indicated, quotations of Harris, Dennett, Dawkins, and Hitchens are from these books.

Chapter 1

1 For John Hick's discussions, see *An Interpretation of Religion* (New Haven, Conn.: Yale University Press, 1988). A good place to begin is his essay "Religious Pluralism and Salvation," *Faith and Philosophy* 5 (1988): 365–77. Also helpful are several of the other essays in the same volume. For D. Z. Phillips' work, see his "Wittgensteinianism: Logic, Reality, and God," in *The Oxford Handbook of Philosophy of Religion*, ed. William Wainwright, 447–71 (Oxford: Oxford University Press, 2005); and D. Z. Phillips, ed., *Wittgenstein and Religion* (New York: Macmillan, 1993).

2 Stephen Jay Gould, *Rocks of Ages: Science and Religion in the Fullness of Life* (New York: Ballantine Books, 1999), 4.

3   Denis Alexander, *Rebuilding the Matrix: Science and Faith in the 21st Century* (Grand Rapids: Zondervan, 2001), 279–80.

4   Denis R. Alexander, "Models for Relating Science and Religion," *Faraday Papers* no. 3 (April 2007): 4. Available online through http://www.faraday-institute.org.

5   See Alister McGrath and Joanna Collicutt McGrath, *The Dawkins Delusion?: Atheist Fundamentalism and the Denial of the Divine* (Downers Grove, Ill.: InterVarsity, 2007), 41.

6   David Hume, *An Enquiry Concerning Human Understanding*, ed. Peter Nidditch, 3rd ed. (Oxford: Oxford University Press, 1975), 115.

7   George I. Mavrodes, "Miracles," in *The Oxford Handbook of Philosophy of Religion*, ed. William J. Wainwright, 308–10 (Oxford: Oxford University Press, 2005).

Chapter 2

1   See A. J. Ayer's classic expression of logical positivism, *Language, Truth, and Logic*, rev. ed. (New York: Dover, 1952). This book was first published in 1936.

2   See Matthew 26:31-35.

3   There are a host of detailed issues that we will not get into here (such as the Gettier-type problems and issues about the degrees of believing). We want to sketch a general account of the role of justification so that we can grasp the role of evidence in *believing that* God exists as well as in *believing in* God.

4   Another view is called *reliabilism*. A reliabilist holds that a belief is justified for a person if that belief was formed by or if it is sustained by belief-forming and -sustaining processes that are generally reliable.

5   The view that belief in God can be justified without evidence has come to be known as *reformed epistemology*. Alvin Plantinga has provided the most sustained defense of this view. To see it in the context of the whole field of epistemology, one ought to consult his "Warrant Trilogy": *Warrant: The Current Debate* (1993), *Warrant and Proper Function* (1993), and *Warranted Christian Belief* (2000), each by Oxford University Press.

6   This distinction can be found in William P. Alston, "Has Foundationalism Been Refuted?" in his *Epistemic Justification: Essays in the Theory of Knowledge*, 39–56 (Ithaca: Cornell University Press, 1989).

7   Translations of *On the Usefulness of Belief* can be found in *Augustine: Earlier Writings*, ed. John Burleigh (Philadelphia: Westminster John Knox, 1953), and in *The Nicene and Post-Nicene Fathers*, vol. 3, ed. Philip Schaff (Grand Rapids: Eerdmans, many editions).

8   Anselm, *Proslogion*, chap. 1, in *Anselm of Canterbury: The Major Works*, ed. Brian Davies and G. R. Evans, Oxford World Classics (Oxford: Oxford University Press, 1998), 87. The quote is from Isaiah 7:9.

9   For Augustine's discussion, see *On Free Choice of the Will*, trans. Thomas Williams (Indianapolis: Hackett, 1993). I do not think that Augustine was successful here, although there are solutions to the problem. It is an instructive case that shows how what seems to generate a conflict between faith and reason might not do so.

Chapter 3

1   Daniel C. Dennett, *Darwin's Dangerous Idea: Evolution and the Meanings of Life* (New York: Simon & Schuster, 1995), chaps. 1 and 7.

2   Aquinas, *Summa Theologiae*, part 1, question 2, article 3, in *Introduction to St. Thomas Aquinas*, ed. Anton C. Pegis (New York: Modern Library, 1945).

3   Aristotle's discussion of his four causes can be found in his *Physics*, book 2, chap. 3.

4   A good study of Aquinas' arguments for God's existence is Anthony Kenny, *The Five Ways: Thomas Aquinas' Proofs of God's Existence* (Notre Dame: University of Notre Dame Press, 1969).

5   See Samuel Clarke, *A Demonstration of the Being and Attributes of God*, ed. Ezio Vailati (Cambridge: Cambridge University Press, 1998); and Gottfried Wilhelm Leibniz, *Principles of Nature and Grace, Based on Reason*, in *Philosophical Essays*, trans. Roger Ariew and Daniel Garber (Indianapolis: Hackett, 1989), 206–13.

6   Peter van Inwagen, *An Essay on Free Will* (Oxford: Oxford University Press, 1983), 202–4. See also van Inwagen, *Metaphysics* (Boulder: Westview, 1993), 104–7.

7   William Lane Craig is the philosopher who has most defended this argument in recent times. Of his many works, see especially *The Kalam Cosmological Argument* (New York: Macmillan, 1979), reprinted by Wipf and Stock, 2000; and William Lane Craig and Quentin Smith, *Theism, Atheism and Big Bang Cosmology* (Oxford: Oxford University Press, 1993).

8   Anselm, *Proslogion*, section 2, in Davies and Evans, *Anselm*, 87 (emphasis in original).

9   Immanual Kant, *Critique of Pure Reason*, trans. and ed. Paul Guyer and Allen W. Wood (Cambridge: Cambridge University Press, 1998), A599/B627, p. 567. Emphasis, which is in italics here, was in bold-faced type in the original. Further references to this source will be cited in the text with the format (Kant, Ax/Bx).

10 Pierre Gassendi, "Fifth Objection," in *The Philosophical Writings of Descartes*, vol. 2, trans. John Cottingham, Robert Stoothoff, and Dugald Murdoch (Cambridge: Cambridge University Press, 1984), 224–25 (AT 323).

11 Descartes, "Fifth Set of Replies," in Cottingham et al., *Philosophical Writings*, 2:262–63 (AT 383).

12 Many scholars think that Anselm put forward a version of this argument based on necessary existence in *Proslogion*, section 3: "And certainly this being so truly exists that it cannot be even thought not to exist. For something can be thought to exist that cannot be thought not to exist, and this is greater than that which can be thought not to exist. Hence, if that-than-which-a-greater-cannot-be-thought can be thought not to exist, then that-than-which-a-greater-cannot-be-thought is not the same as that-than-which-a-greater-cannot-be-thought, which is absurd."

13 Gaunilo of Marmoutiers, "*Pro Insipiente* (On Behalf of the Fool)," in Davies and Evans, *Anselm*, 105–10. Anselm's reply to Gaunilo is found on pp. 111–22.

14 The phrase "great-making properties" is from Alvin Plantinga, *God, Freedom, and Evil* (Grand Rapids: Eerdmans, 1974), 98.

15 For Kant's discussion of these terms, see the *Critique of Pure Reason*, B1–24.

16 The claim that the propositions of arithmetic and geometry are synthetic is quite controversial in philosophy. I do not mean to endorse this claim. I am giving background to Kant's statements that relate to Dennett's concerns.

17 For a clear articulation of this line of thinking, see C. S. Lewis, "Right and Wrong as a Clue to the Meaning of the Universe," part 1 of *Mere Christianity* (New York: Touchstone, 1996). I included a basic sort of moral argument in my *Thinking about God: First Steps in Philosophy* (Downers Grove, Ill.: InterVarsity, 2004), chaps. 14 and 15.

18 There is actually a good deal of empirical evidence that the more religious one is, the more generous one will be. See, e.g., Arthur C. Brooks, *Who Really Cares: The Surprising Truth about Compassionate Conservatism* (New York: Basic Books, 2006); Jonathan Haidt, "Moral Psychology and the Misunderstanding of Religion," found online at http://www.edge.org/3rd_culture/haidt07/haidt07_index.html.

19 George I. Mavrodes, "Religion and the Queerness of Morality," in *Rationality, Religious Belief, and Moral Commitment: New Essays in the Philosophy of Religion*, ed. Robert Audi and William J. Wainwright (Ithaca: Cornell University Press, 1986), 213–26. The citation from Bertrand

Russell is from "A Free Man's Worship," in *Mysticism and Logic* (New York: Barnes & Noble, 1917), 47.

20   In "Necessary Moral Truths and the Need for Explanation," *Philosophia Christi*, ser. 2, 2, no. 1 (2000): 105–12, I propose a different sort of argument for God's existence, beginning with the notion that moral obligations are necessary truths similar to Platonic forms.

21   John L. Mackie, *The Miracle of Theism: Arguments for and against the Existence of God* (Oxford: Clarendon, 1982), 115–16.

22   Ganssle, *Thinking about God*, chap. 15, pp. 97–103. The following several paragraphs are drawn from this chapter.

23   Immanuel Kant's moral philosophy also is developed in terms of the categorical imperative. He first recognizes that the concept of moral obligation takes the form of categorical imperative. He then derives what he takes to be the foundational rule or criterion for moral decisions from pure reason. This criterion is what he calls the categorical imperative. In this section, we are drawing on his analysis of the concept of moral obligation, but we are not deriving any criterion for determining which actions are morally permitted. In the context of the argument, we are more interested in the structure of the commands themselves. For Kant's view, see *Grounding for the Metaphysics of Morals*, trans. James Ellington (Indianapolis: Hackett, 1993).

24   This claim has to do with the moral point of view. It is not that some *particular* moral rule is itself absolute and unconditional. For example, it may be that there are circumstances that justify lying. One who does so in these cases has not rejected the moral game. She has applied her best thinking to the situation, and she has concluded that her unconditional moral obligations do not prohibit lying in that particular situation.

Chapter 4

1   William Paley, *Natural Theology* (Boston: Marsh, Capen, Lyon, & Webb, 1839), 1:49–50 (emphasis in original). This work was originally published in 1802. Further references to this work will be cited parenthetically as (Paley, volume:page).

2   David Hume, *Dialogues Concerning Natural Religion*, ed. Norman Kemp Smith, 2nd ed. (London: Thomas Nelson, 1947), 2:147. Further references to this work will be cited parenthetically as (Part, page).

3   For more detailed discussion of the various laws and physical constants that enter into fine-tuning arguments, see Robin Collins, "Evidence for Fine-Tuning," in *God and Design: The Teleological Argument and Modern Science*, ed. Neil A. Manson, 178–99 (London: Routledge, 2003); and John Leslie, *Universes* (London: Routledge, 1989), chap. 2.

4   van Inwagen, *Metaphysics*, 136.
5   John D. Barrow and Frank J. Tipler, *The Anthropic Cosmological Principle* (Oxford: Oxford University Press, 1986), 21.
6   Brandon Carter, "Large Number Coincidences and the Anthropic Principle in Cosmology," in *Confrontation of Cosmological Theories with Observational Data*, ed. S. M. Longair (Dordrecht: Reidel, 1974), 291–98. The citation is from pages 295–96 (emphasis in original).
7   Dennett cites Smolin's paper, "Did the Universe Evolve?" in *Classical and Quantum Gravity* 9 (1992): 173–91; Dawkins refers to Smolin's book, *The Life of the Cosmos* (London: Weidenfeld & Nicolson, 1997).
8   William Lane Craig, "Design and the Anthropic Fine-Tuning of the Universe," in Manson, *God and Design*, 155–77 (citation from 171).
9   Robin Collins, "The Teleological Argument," in *The Rationality of Theism*, ed. Paul Copan and Paul Moser, 132–48 (London: Routledge, 2003, citation from 143.
10 Martin Rees, "Other Universes: A Scientific Perspective," in Manson, *God and Design*, 211–20 (citation from 214).
11 Roger White, "Fine-Tuning and Multiple Universes," in Manson, *God and Design*, 229–50.

Chapter 5

1   Dennett himself introduced and developed the notion of the intentional stance in a variety of papers and in the book *The Intentional Stance* (Cambridge, Mass.: MIT Press, 1987).
2   Richard Dawkins, *The Selfish Gene* (Oxford: Oxford University Press, 1976).
3   *The Chronicles of Narnia: The Lion, the Witch, and the Wardrobe*. Dir. Andrew Adamson, Buena Vista Film, 2005.
4   There are many good translations of *On the Genealogy of Morality* available, including the one edited by Keith Ansell-Pearson (Cambridge: Cambridge University Press, 1994).

Chapter 6

1   Anthony Flew, *The Presumption of Atheism*, originally published under this title by Pemberton Publishing in 1976, republished as *God, Freedom, and Immortality: A Critical Analysis* (Buffalo: Prometheus Books, 1984).
2   The literature on the problem of evil is immense. In the preface to his edited collection, *The Evidential Argument from Evil* (Bloomington: Indiana University Press, 1996), Daniel Howard-Snyder reports that over

4,200 philosophical and theological items were published on the problem of evil between 1960 and 1990. Many more have been published since then. The free will defense is best articulated by Plantinga. See his *God*, 7–64; and *The Nature of Necessity* (Oxford: Oxford University Press, 1974), 165–95. For my contribution to the discussion, see my "God and Evil," in Copan and Moser, *Rationality*, 259–77.

3   William Rowe, "The Problem of Evil and Some Varieties of Atheism," *American Philosophical Quarterly* 16 (1979): 335–41; repr. in Howard-Snyder, *Evidential Argument* 1–11.

4   The following few pages follow closely my "God and Evil," in Copan and Moser, *Rationality*, 259–77.

5   See Stephen J. Wykstra, "The Humean Obstacle to Evidential Arguments from Suffering: On Avoiding the Evils of 'Appearance,'" *International Journal for the Philosophy of Religion* 16 (1974): 73–93.

6   For discussion of other forms of the evidential problem of evil, see my "God and Evil," in Copan and Moser, *Rationality* and the literature cited there.

Chapter 7

1   Robert Van Gulick lists seven features of consciousness, including the qualitative character of conscious experience, the phenomenal structure, the intrinsic subjectivity of consciousness, the self-perspectival organization, and the unity of conscious experience. See Van Gulick, "Consciousness," *The Stanford Encyclopedia of Philosophy*, ed. Edward N. Zalta, http://plato.stanford.edu/entries/consciousness/#4.

2   To be sure, we do not know directly all of our mental states. We do have privileged access to some of them.

3   In fact, Daniel Dennett has spent a good part of his career trying to develop a naturalistic theory of consciousness and intentionality. See, e.g., *Content and Consciousness* (London: Routledge & Kegan Paul, 1969); and *Consciousness Explained* (Boston: Little, Brown, 1991).

4   The following discussion owes much to cautions and suggestions put forward in conversation by Bill Alston.

5   There are some who do argue in this way. See, e.g., J. P. Moreland, "The Argument from Consciousness," in Copan and Moser, *Rationality*, 204–20; and *Consciousness and the Existence of God*, Routledge Studies in the Philosophy of Religion (London: Routledge, 2008). See also Charles Taliaferro, "Naturalism and the Mind," in *Naturalism: A Critical Analysis*, ed. William Lane Craig and J. P. Moreland, 133–55 (London: Routledge, 2000).

6   David J. Chalmers, "Facing Up to the Problem of Consciousness," *Journal of Consciousness Studies* 2, no. 3 (1995): 200–219 (available on the Web through http://www.imprint.co.uk); and *The Conscious Mind* (New York: Oxford University Press, 1996).
7   An example is Derk Pereboom. See his *Living without Free Will* (Cambridge: Cambridge University Press, 2001).
8   For examples of the compatibilists, see the many essays in *The Oxford Companion to Free Will*, ed. Robert Kane (Oxford: Oxford University Press, 2001). Daniel Dennett's work on human freedom is *Elbow Room: The Varieties of Free Will Worth Wanting* (Cambridge, Mass.: MIT Press, 1984).
9   Others who make similar arguments include Peter Unger, "Free Will and Scientificalism," *Philosophy and Phenomenological Research* 65 (2002): 1–25; and Stewart Goetz, "Naturalism and Libertarian Agency," in Craig and Moreland, *Naturalism*, 156–86.
10   Mackie, *Miracle*, 115–16.
11   Paul Draper, e-mail correspondence, October 28, 1999. Cited in Gregory E. Ganssle, "Necessary Moral Truths and the Need for Explanation," *Philosophia Christi*, ser. 2, 2, no. 1 (2000): 105–12.

Index